RED HOT WEST
KARIJINI

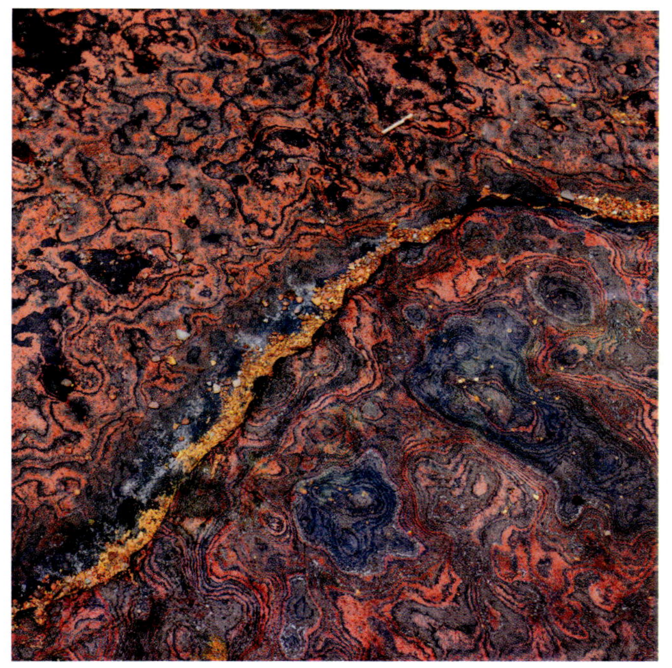

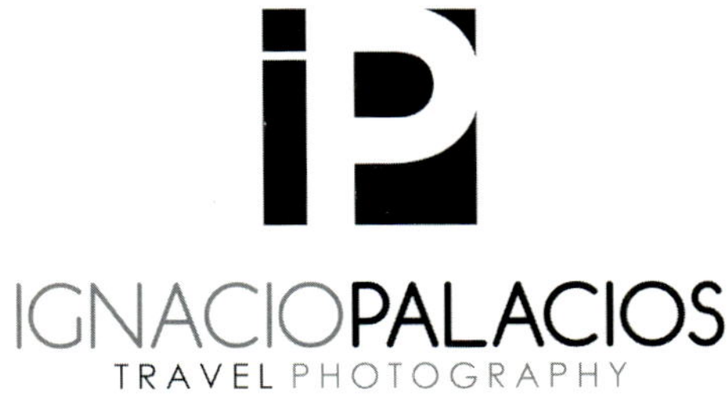

IGNACIO PALACIOS
TRAVEL PHOTOGRAPHY

First Published in 2013 by Ignacio Palacios Photography

National Library of Australian Cataloguing-in-Publication data
Author: Ignacio Palacios, 1974
Title: Red Hot West: Karijini
ISBN: 978-0-646-59061-5

Photography by Ignacio Palacios, www.iptravelphotography.com.au
Text edited by Lucinda Murray
Designed by Vanesa Wilton, www.billyboydesign.com.au
Book layout, image preparation/editing by Ignacio Palacios

Printed in China through Asia Pacific Offset Limited

Cover Image: Dales Gorge

info@iptravelphotography.com.au
www.iptravelphotography.com.au

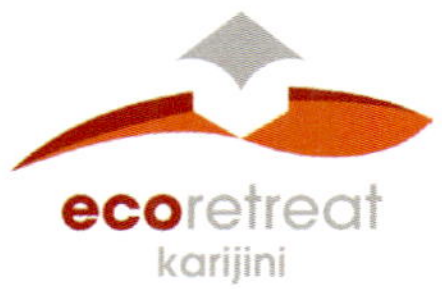

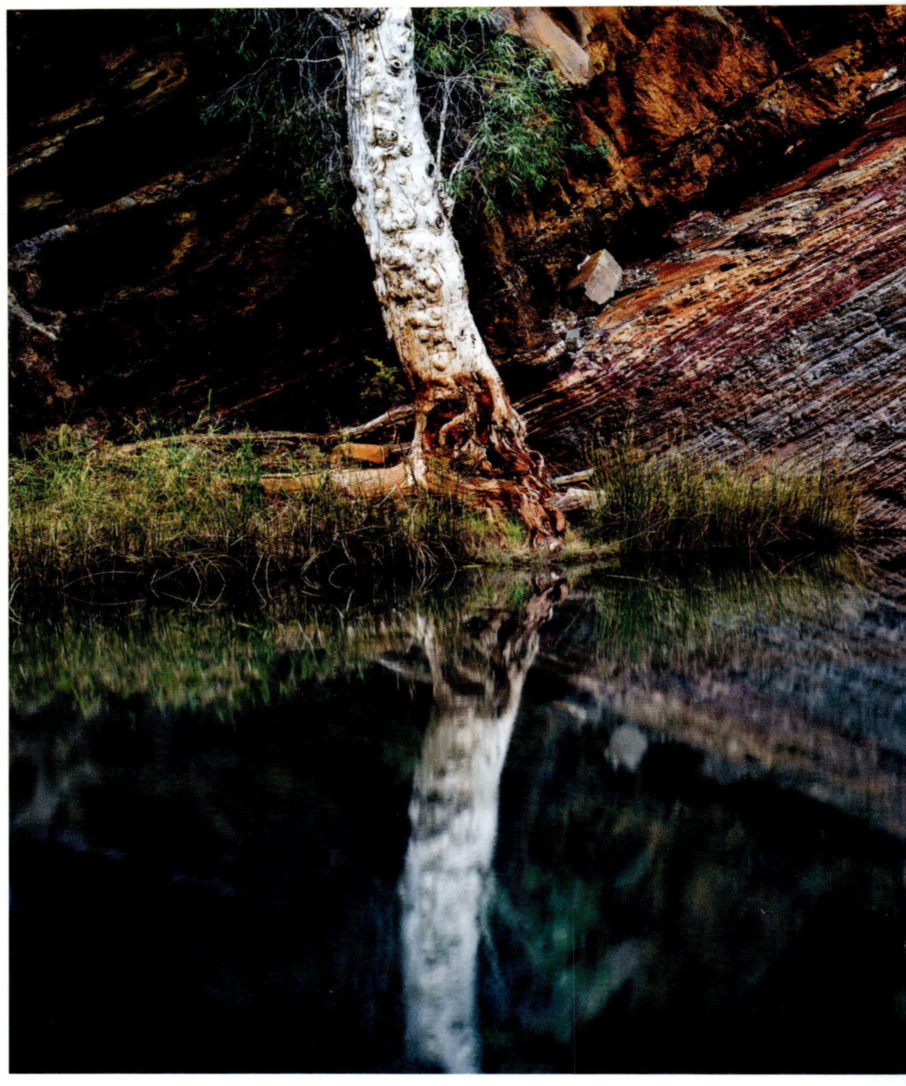
HAMERSLEY GORGE

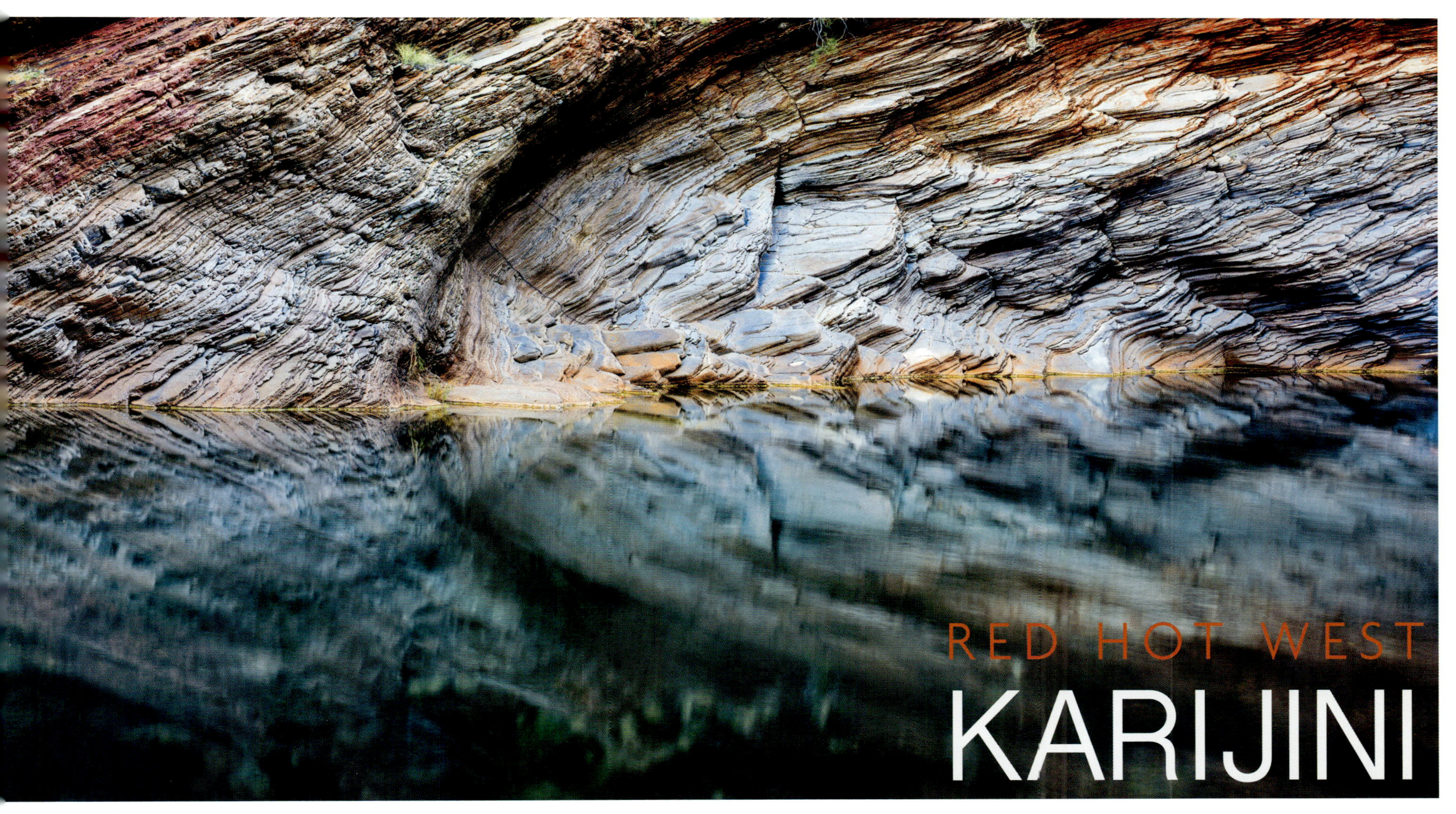

PHOTOGRAPHS BY IGNACIO PALACIOS

Since I came to Australia four years ago, I had always dreamt about going to Karijini National Park. I had seen great panoramic photographs by Ken Duncan and I was wondering if those beautifully saturated colors where actually real.

I knew it was a very photogenic and special place so I decided to join Peter Eastway, Christian Fletcher and Tony Hewitt's workshop for five days to discover the park and learn some tricks from the masters.

I have been lucky to get enough good pictures to make an exhibition and a book in just one trip but the nine days I spent in the park where pretty intense. I was waking up at 5 am to arrive to the gorges and lookouts just in time to get ready and capture the sunrise light. A few days, I arrived to the resort so late that the kitchen was already closed and I had to satisfy with a tin of red beans. Between the sunrise and sunset, temperatures were unbearable and I spent hours in the shade of the resort retouching photographs.

After the photography workshop, I stayed another four days and went back to some locations to continue shooting at the most special places. This time I was alone in the gorges and it gave me a lot more time and flexibility to concentrate on composition and getting the perfect shot. I went to Hamersley gorge, Mt Bruce, Forstescue falls, Circular and Fern pools to complete my work of photographing the park.

This area of Australia, together with the Kimberley is one of the most special places I have ever seen in my travels.

For my wife, Lucy for showing me this beautiful country and supporting and believing in my dreams. For my sons Rafa and Leo with whom I will visit this beautiful National Park when they are old enough to swim in the gorges.

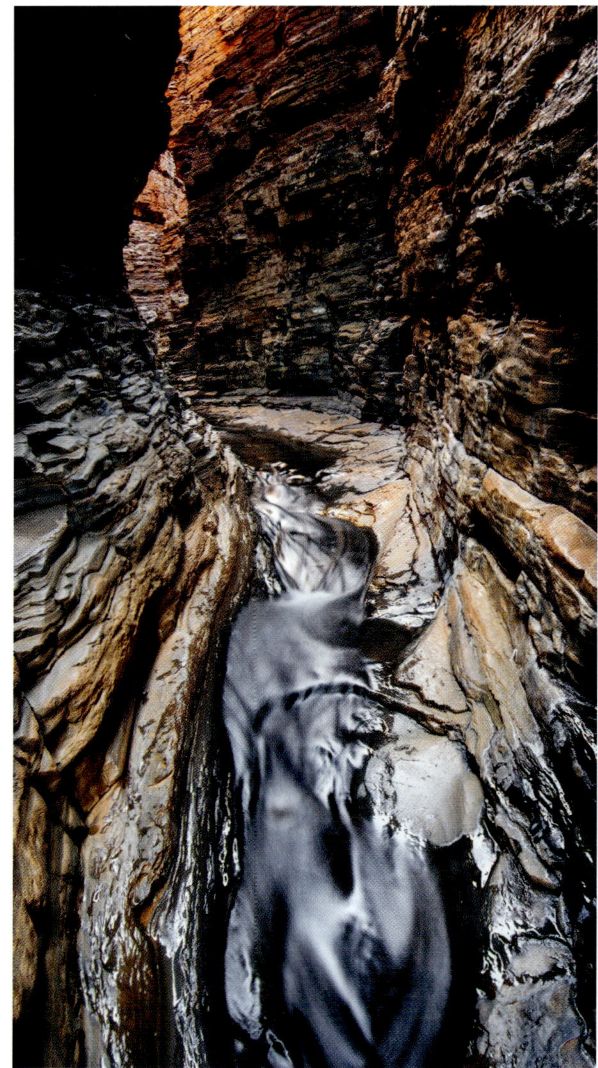

Contents

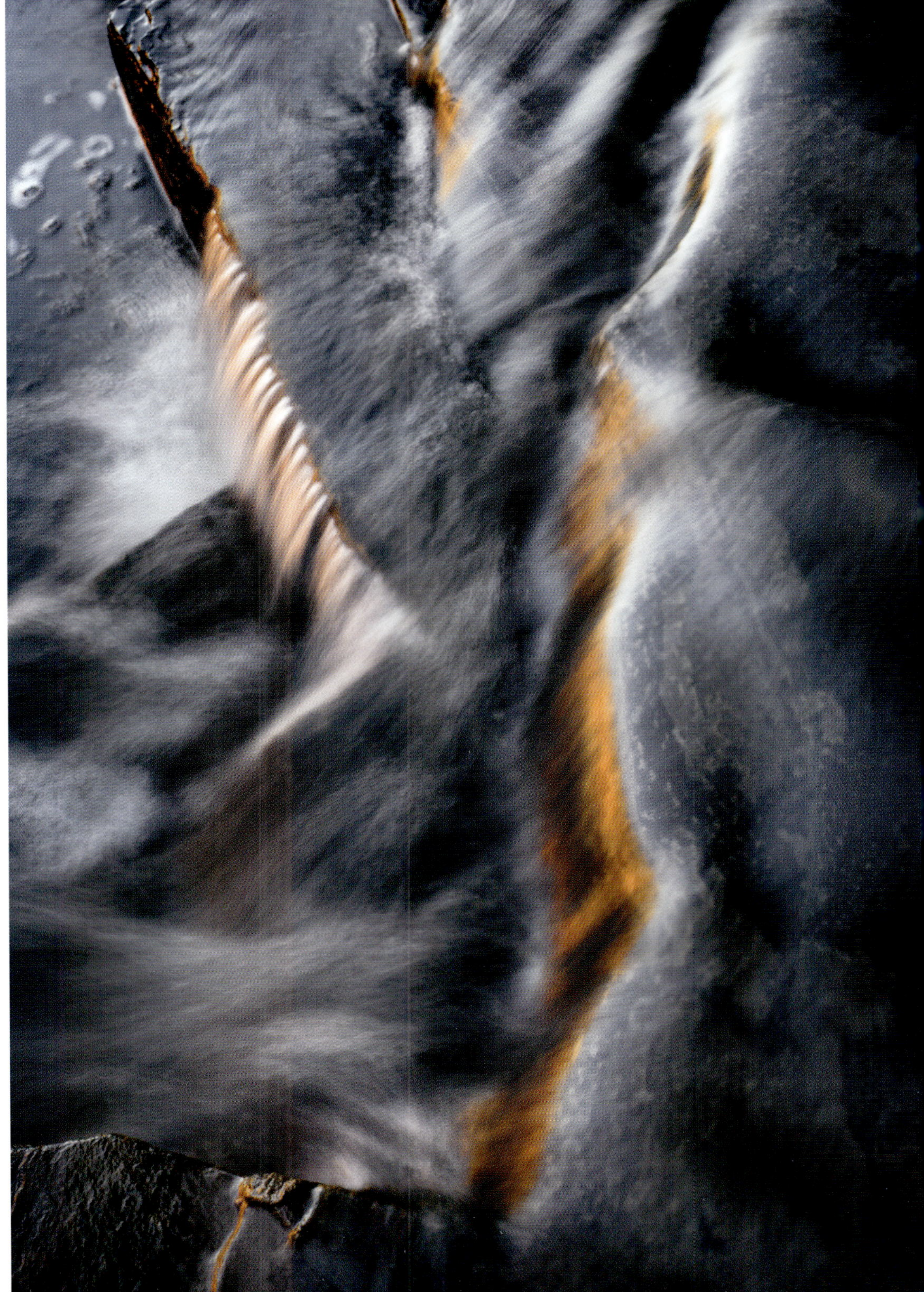

KALAMINA GORGE

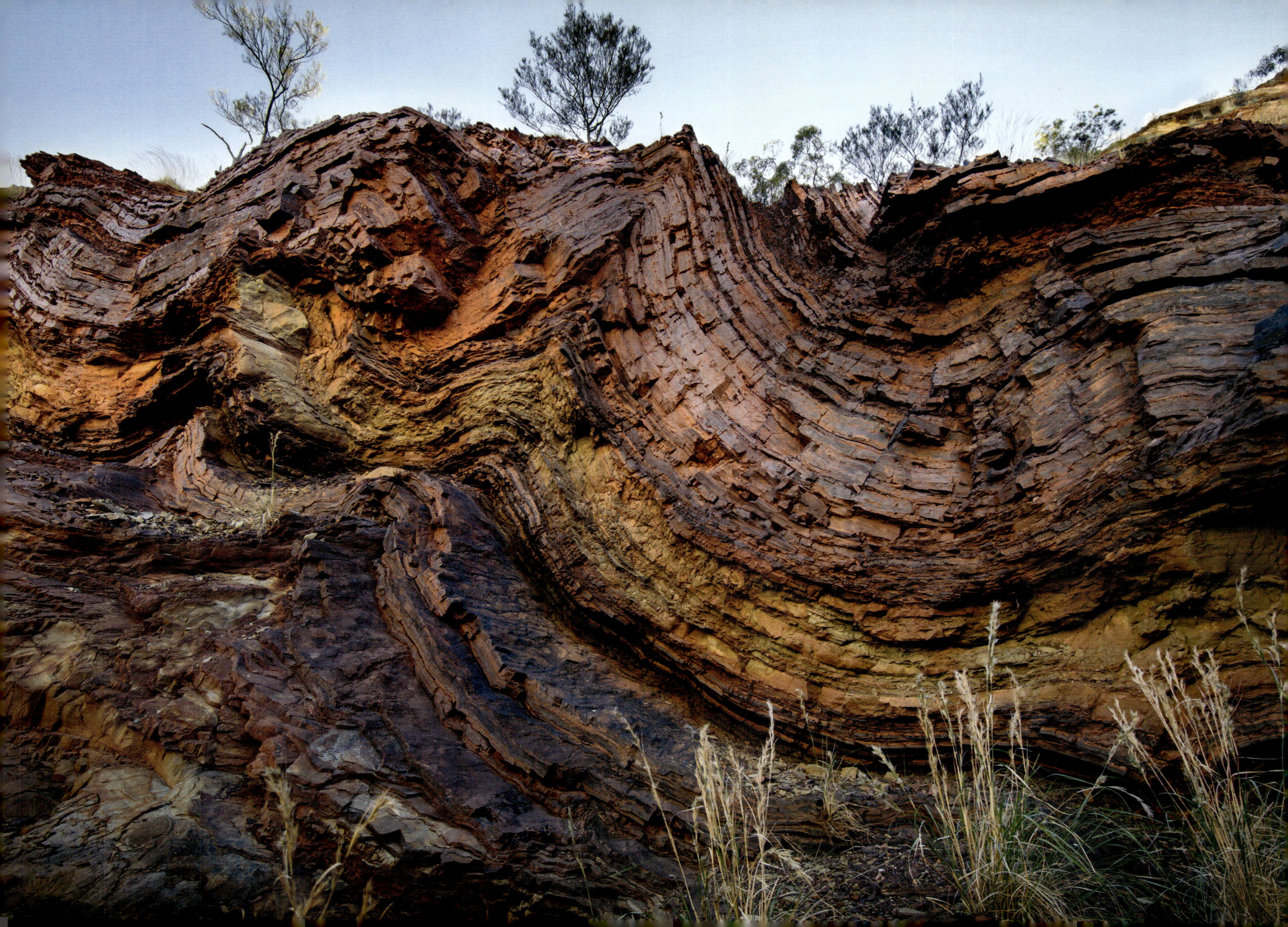

Karijini National Park in Western Australia is one of the largest and most photogenic National Parks in Australia. The park is famous for its sheer gorges, waterfalls, sparkling rock pools and cool swimming holes. Still it remains relatively unknown on the east coast. Karijini is about 275km south of Port Hedland and 100km east of Tom Price or Paraburdoo.

The park is all about exploring serpentine tunnels of marbled rock, clambering over boulders, squeezing through narrow tunnels, inching your way along ledges, paddling through subterranean waterways and descending deep into chasms which have been eroded into the landscape over two billion years.

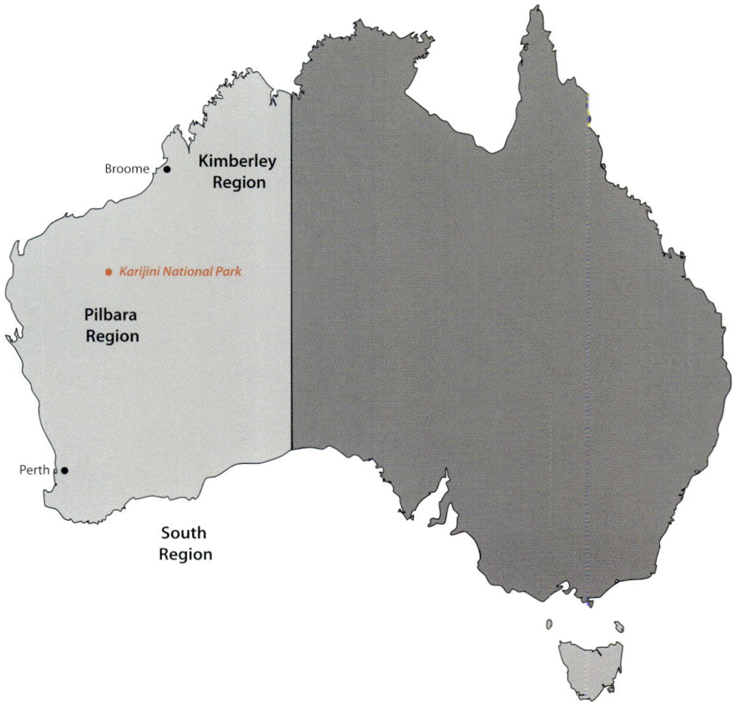

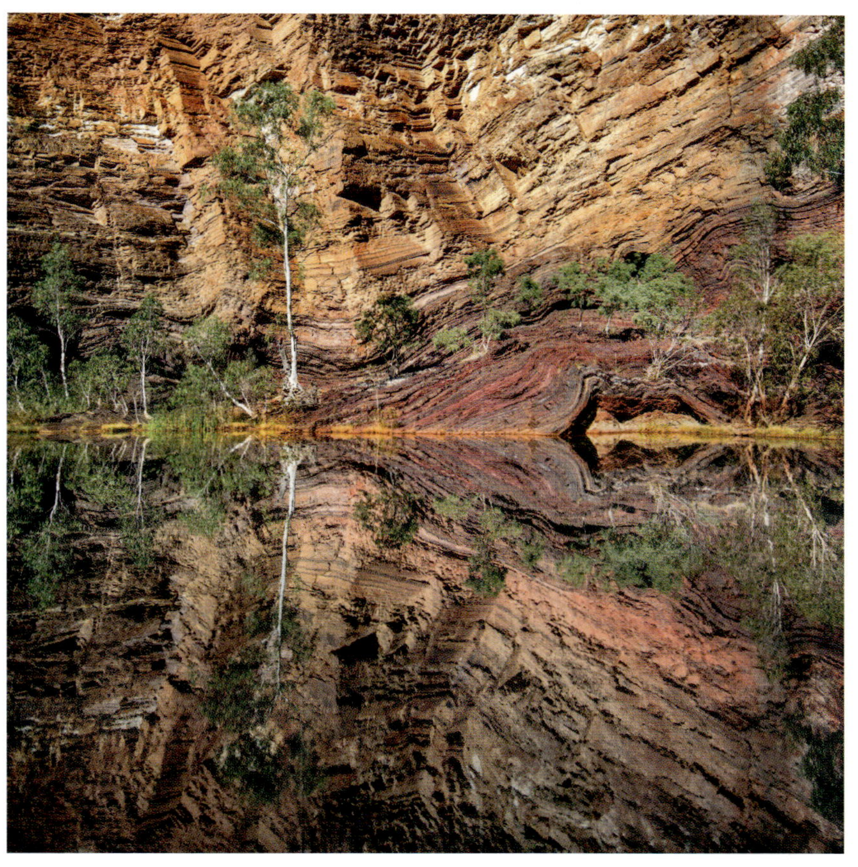

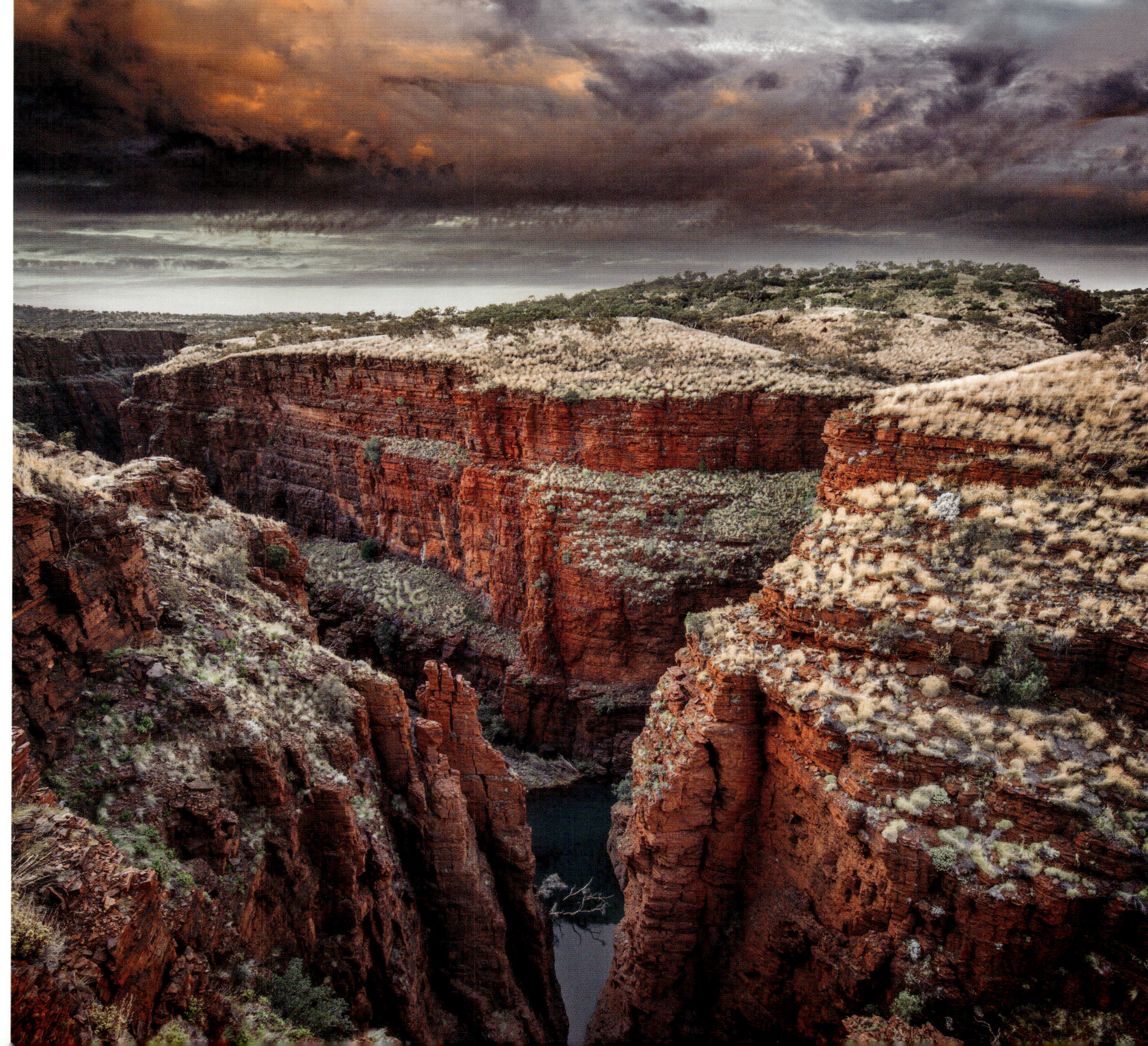

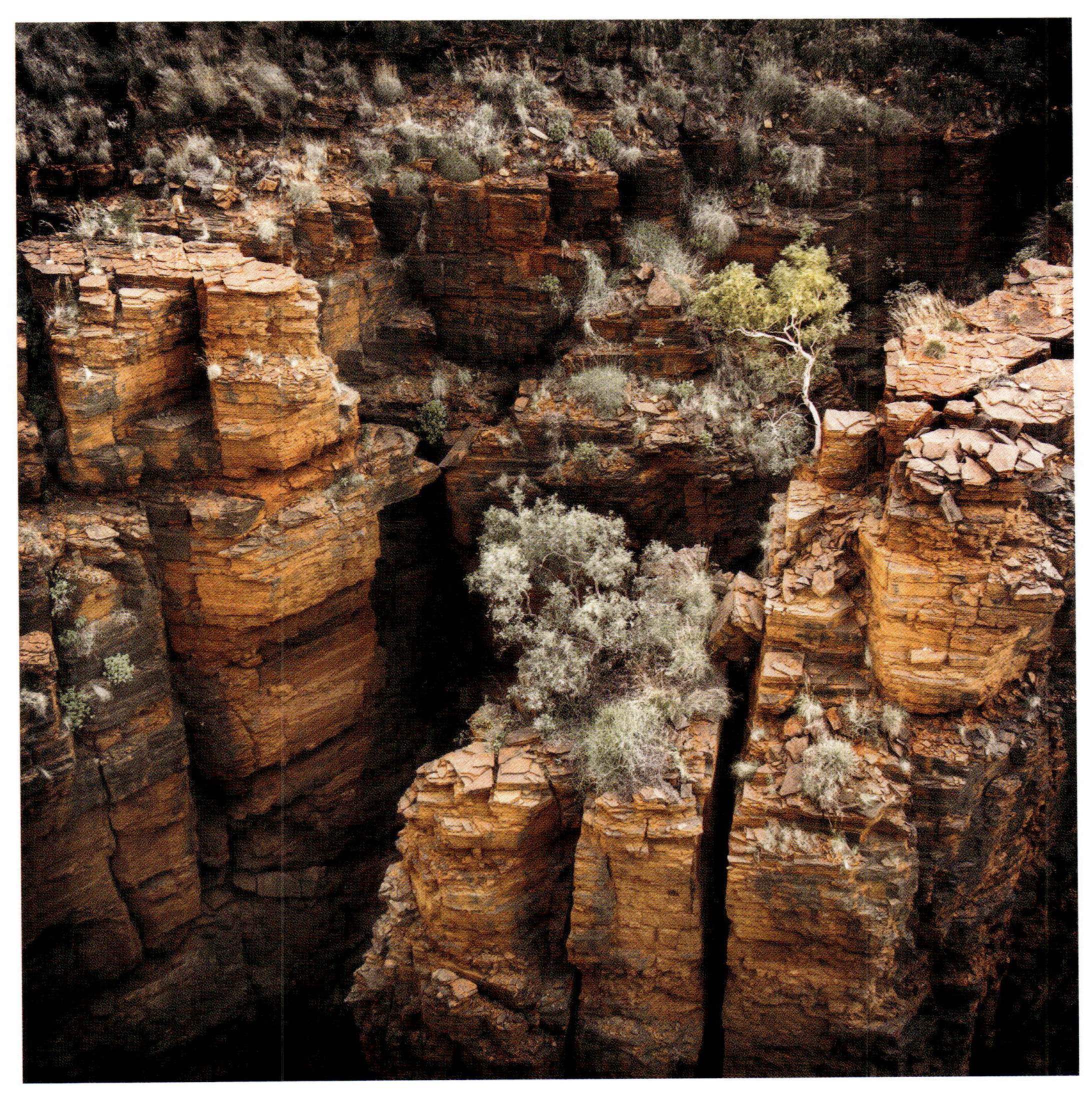

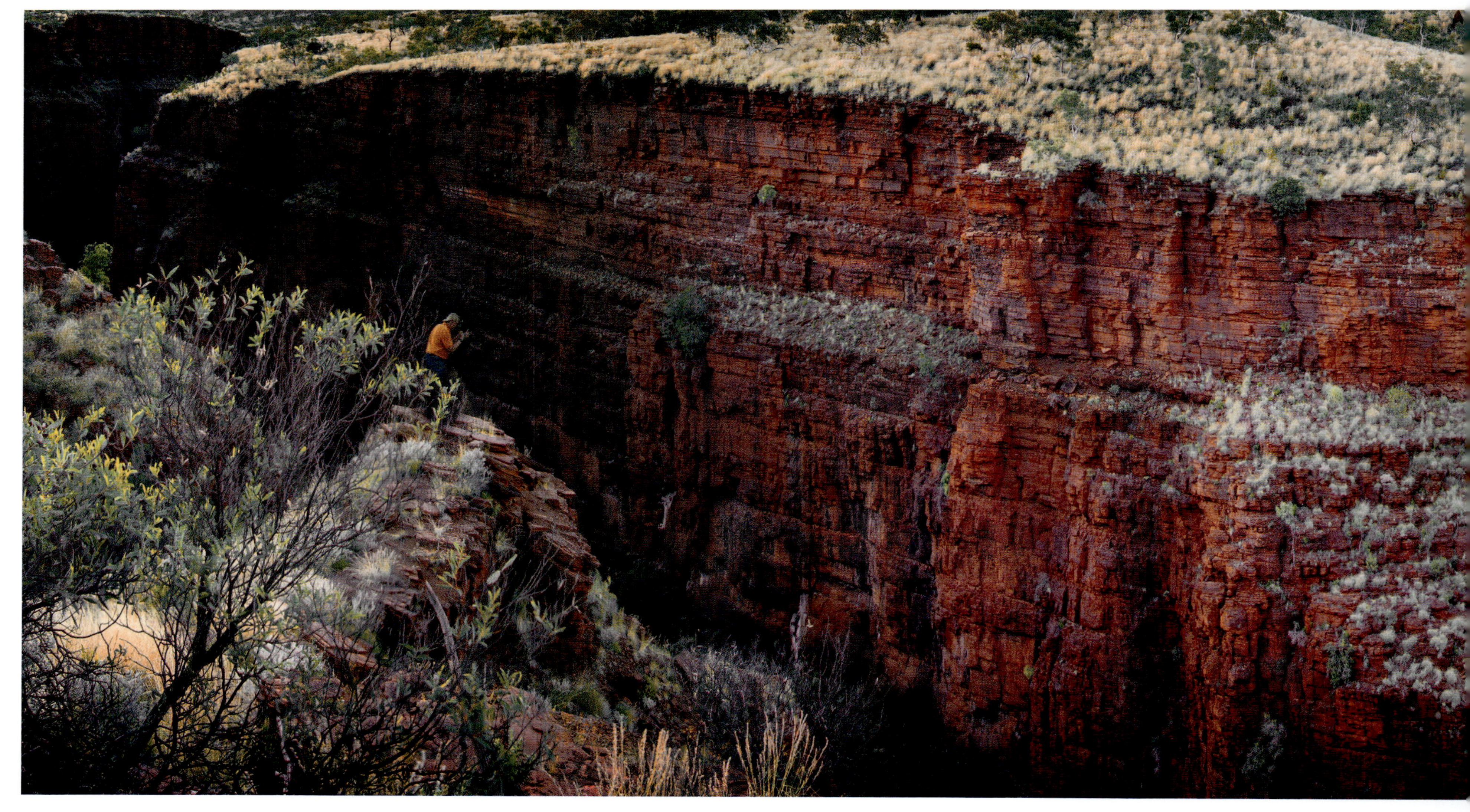

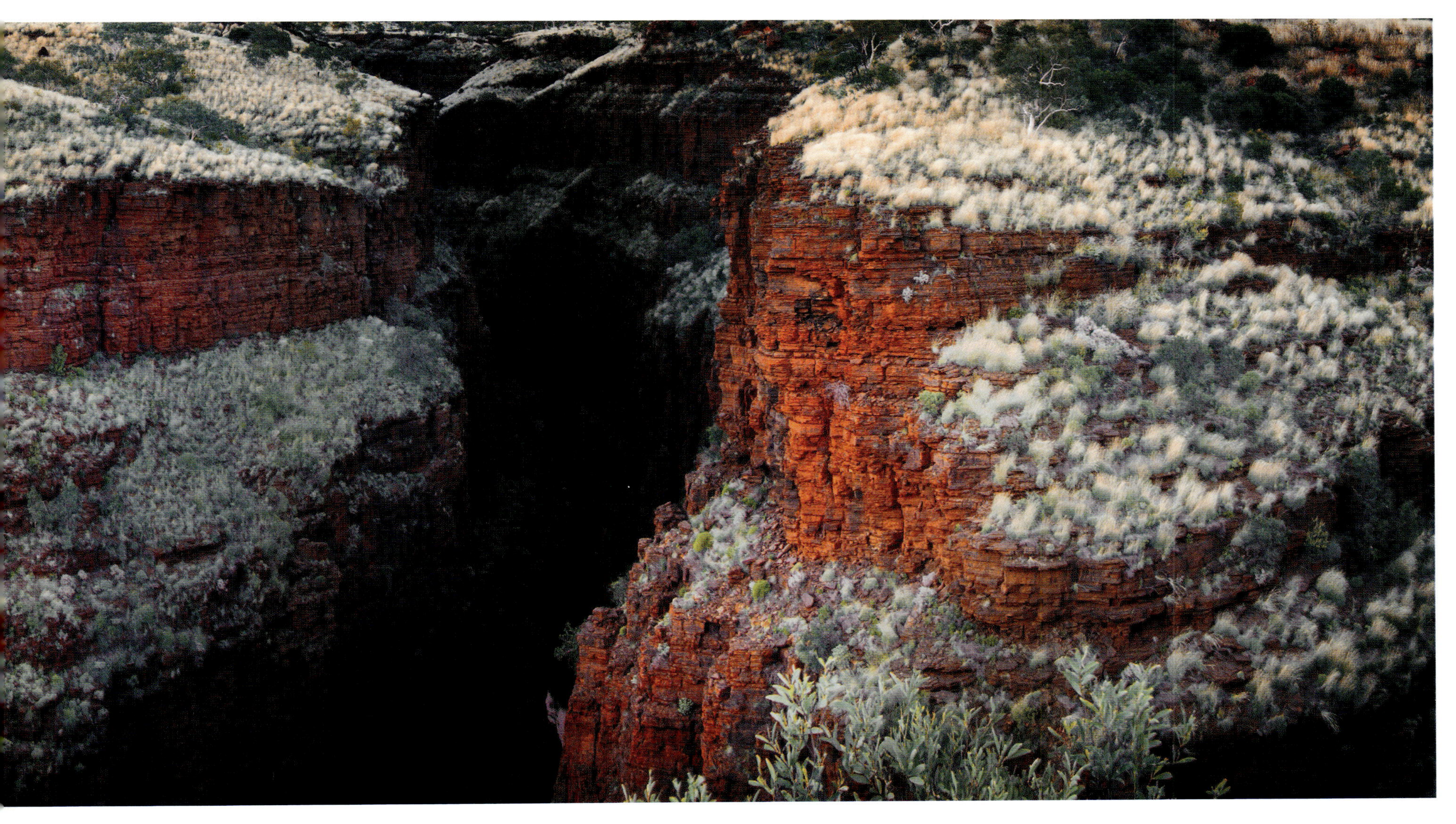

Oxer Lookout is the most spectacular sight in the Pilbara and possibly the most stunning lookout in Australia. It celebrates the junction of four mighty gorges: Red, Weano, Joffre and Hancock gorges. This photograph was taken during sunrise.

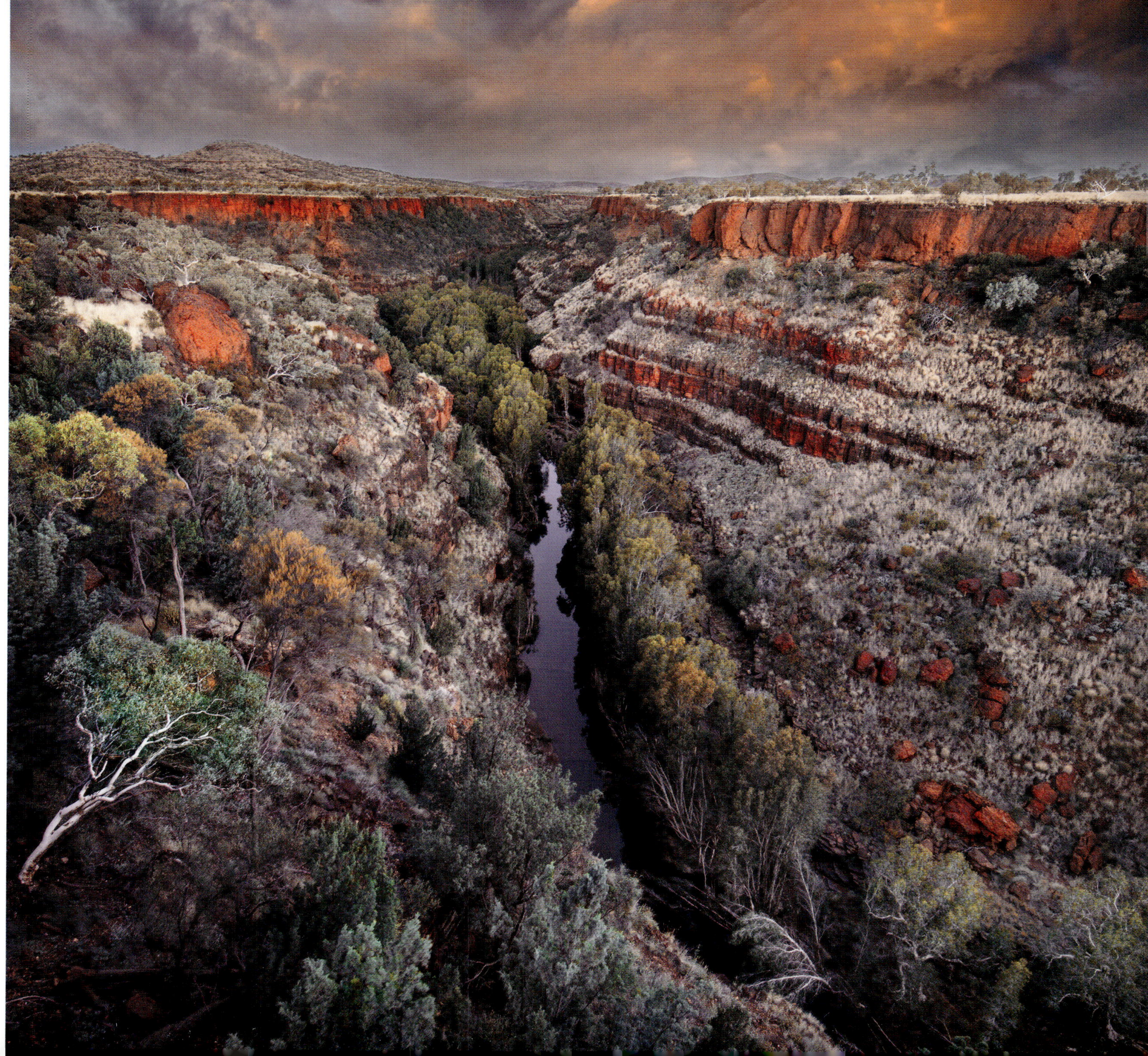

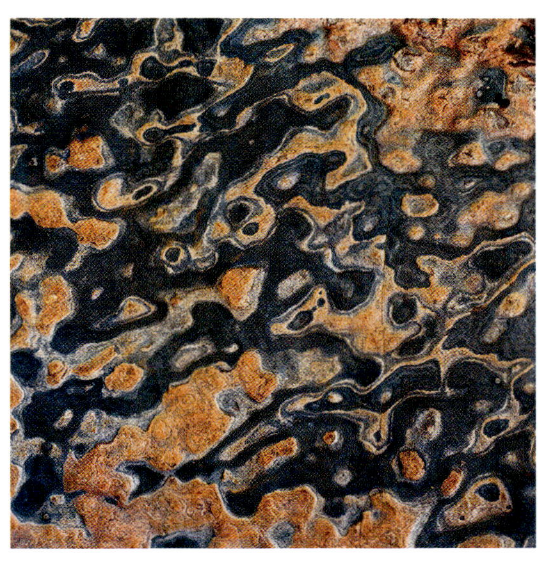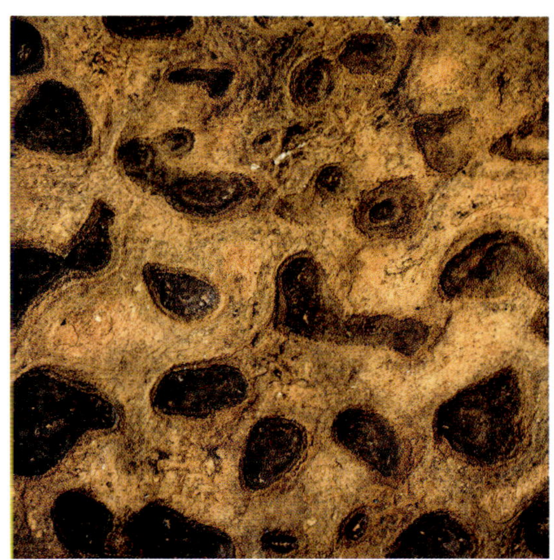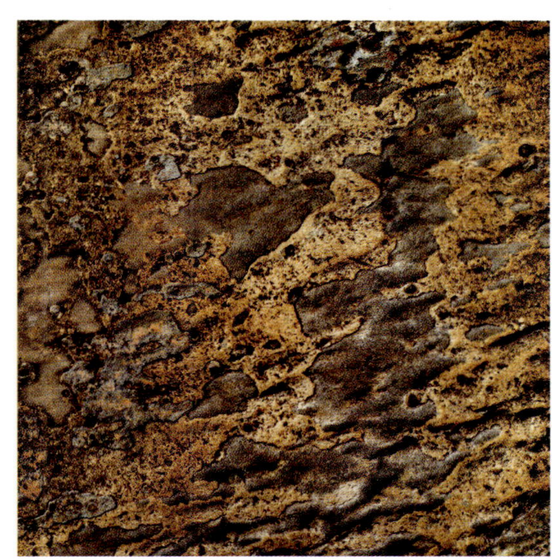

Dales Gorge, Three Way Lookout

(opposite page) This photograph was taken at sunset. I discovered the lookout during the day and came back to the same location to take the photograph at sunset when the light is at its best. I was rewarded with a beautiful sunset. After taking the picture I then learnt that this is a famous lookout called Three Ways Lookout. I was the only one there for hours, waiting for the light.

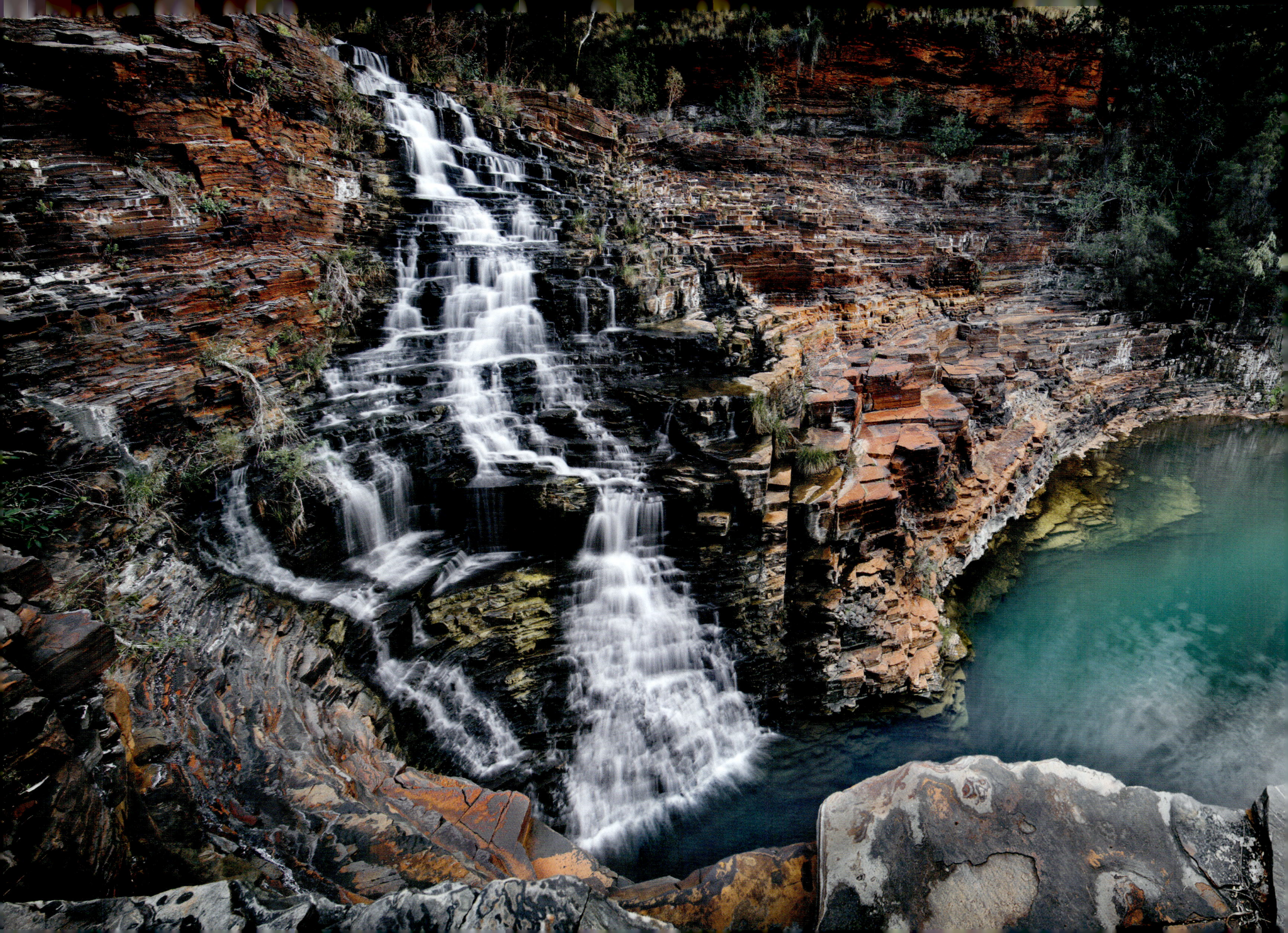

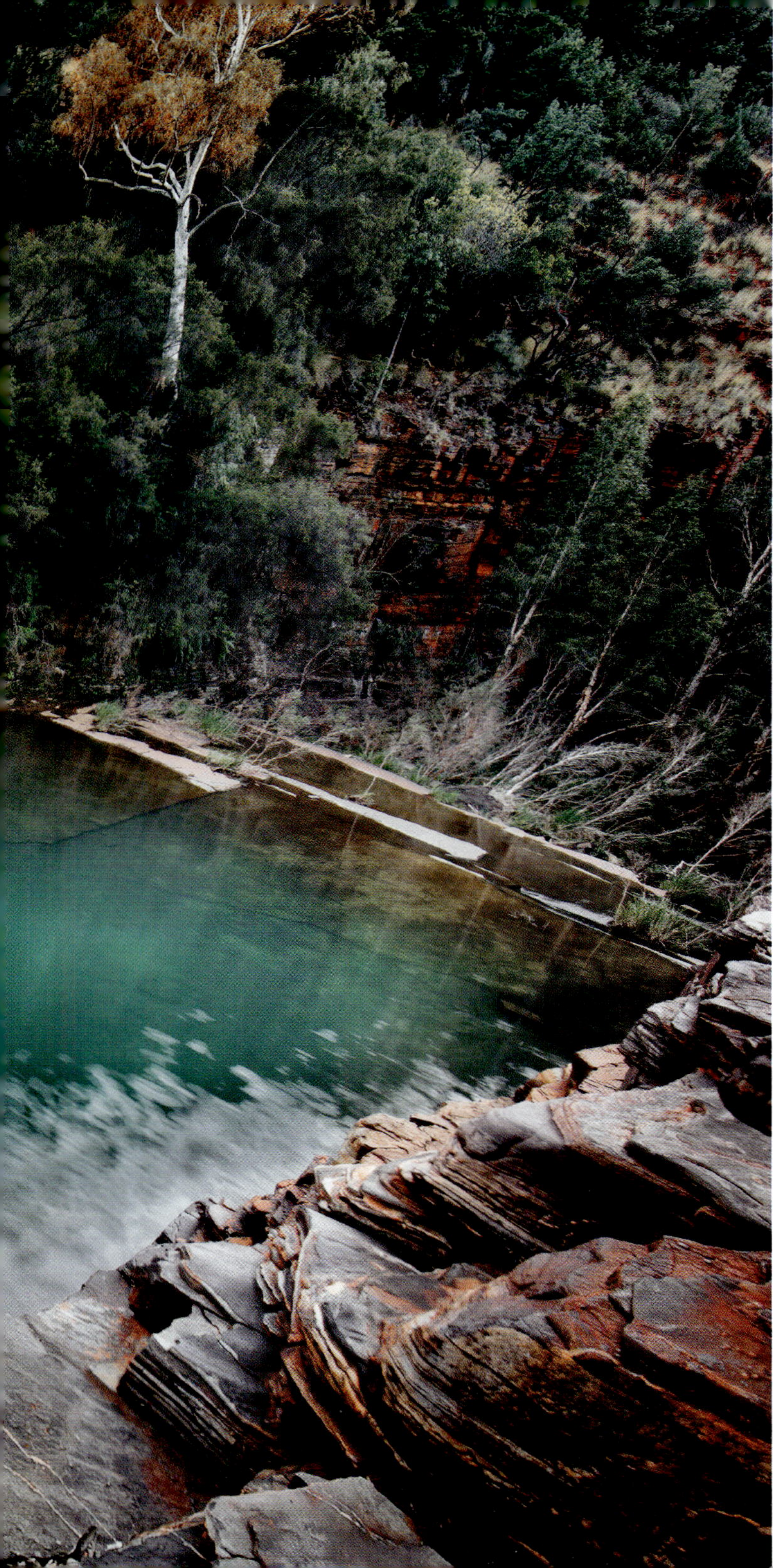

Dales Gorge, Fortescue Falls

Fortescue Falls is one of the highlights of Dales Gorge. This photograph had to be taken very early in the morning since the gorge is very wide and the sun starts to hit the water quite strongly right after sunrise. There was a little bit of climbing involved with heavy equipment in my bag but the shot was worth it. This photograph is a stitched panorama made up of four shots.

I had to wake up really early in the morning to take this picture. The first time I arrived at 6.15 am and it was already too late as the sun was hitting the top part of the falls so I could only photograph the bottom part (page 17).

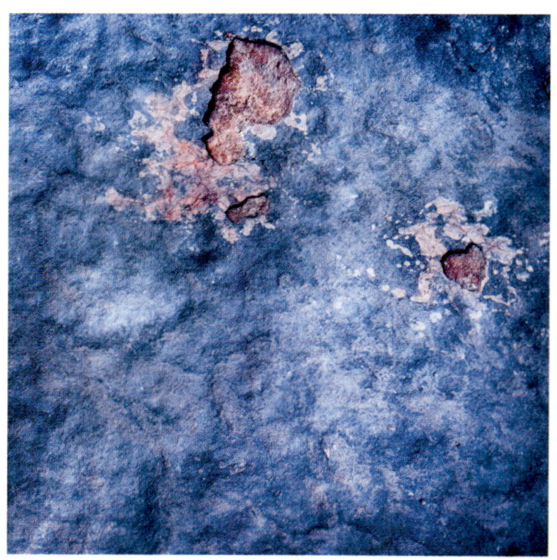 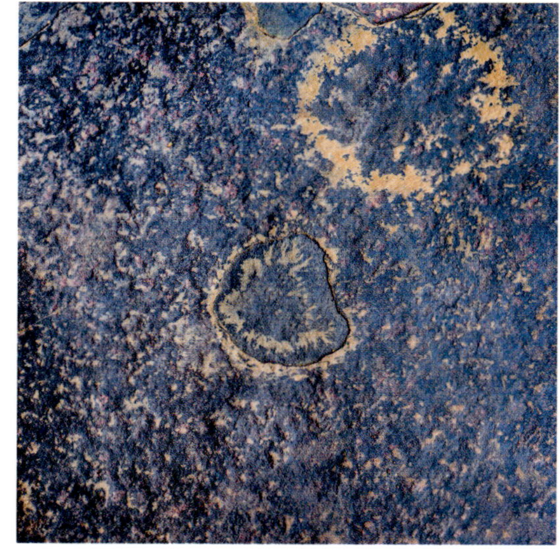 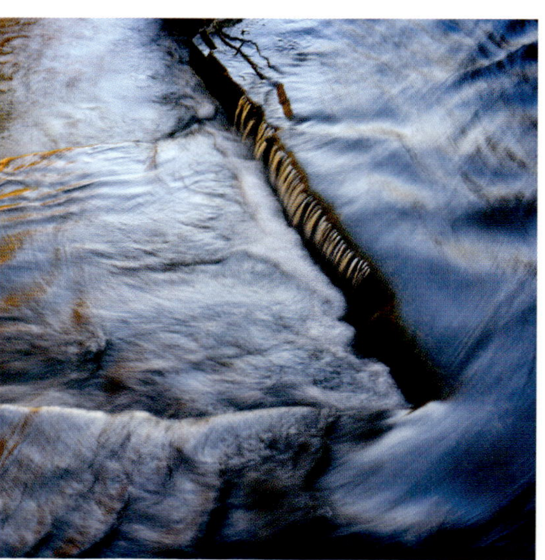

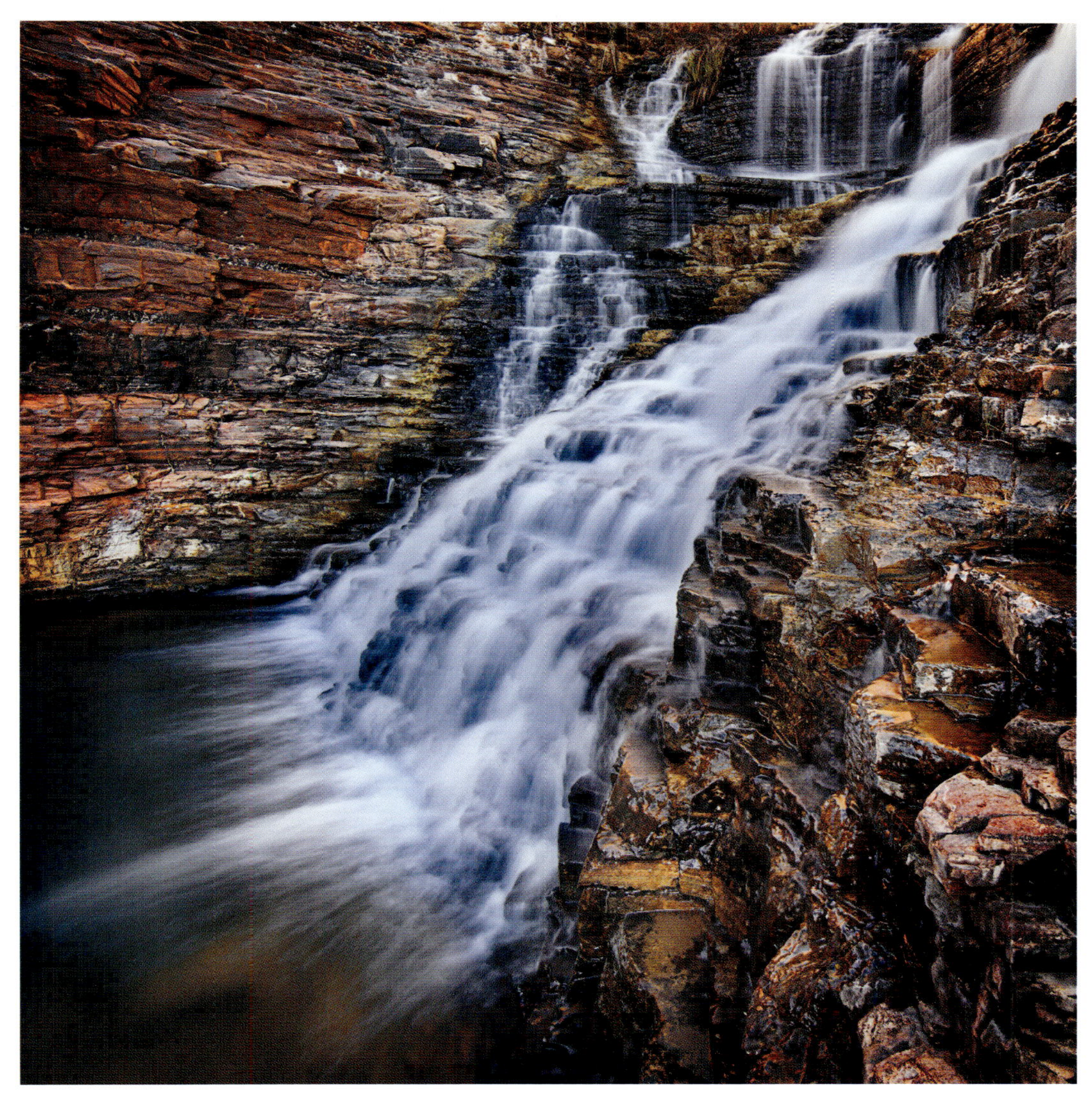

Hancock Gorge, Kermits Pool

Karijini has a system of excellent walking trails of varying degrees of difficulty which will lead you deep into the subterranean gorges and through waterfalls where you can dive into sparkling rock pools. Hancock is one of the most spectacular gorges. After climbing down a ladder, you wander into the gorge which narrows into a huge chamber and an attractive setting of small rock pools and marbled walls.

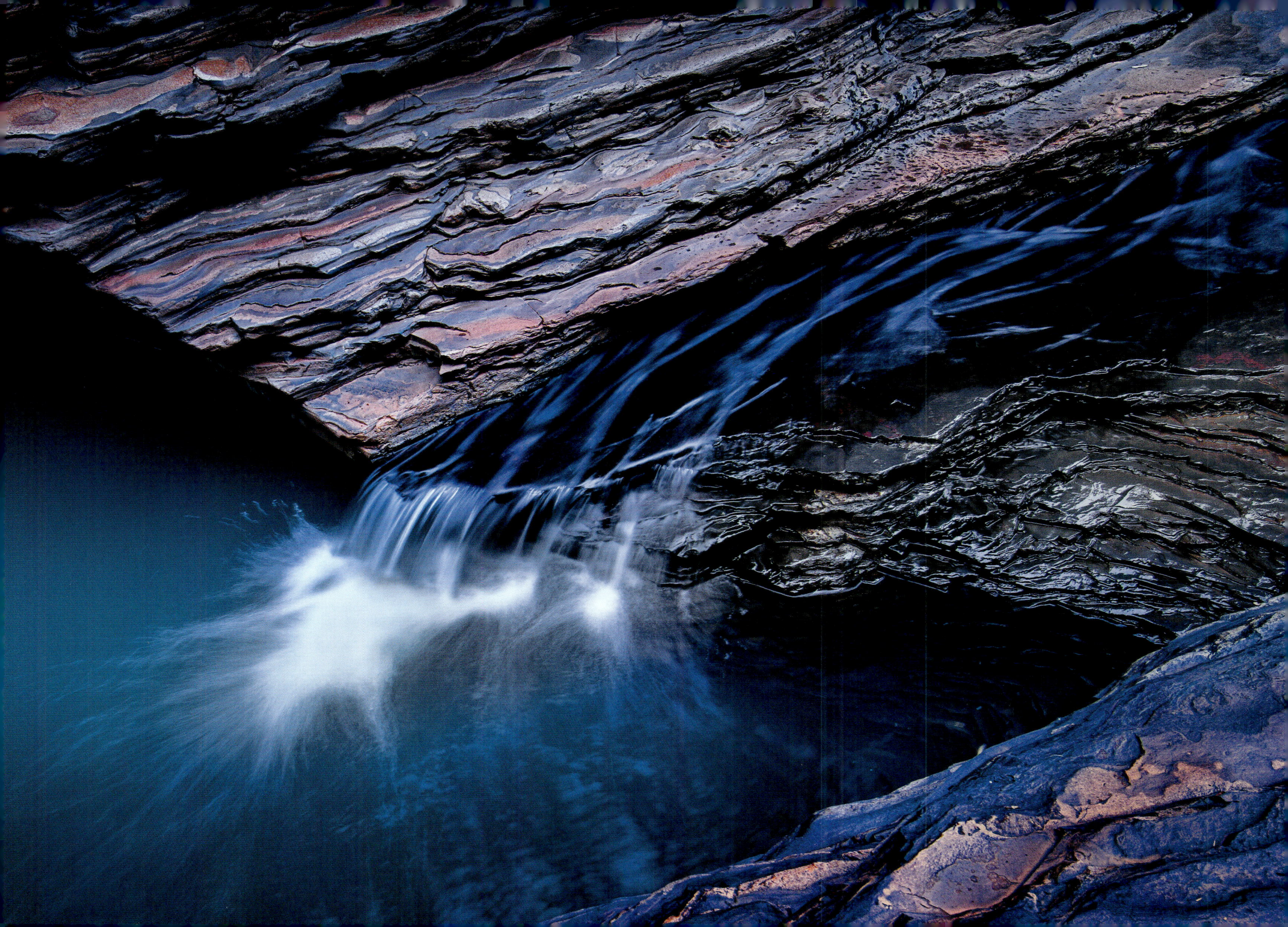

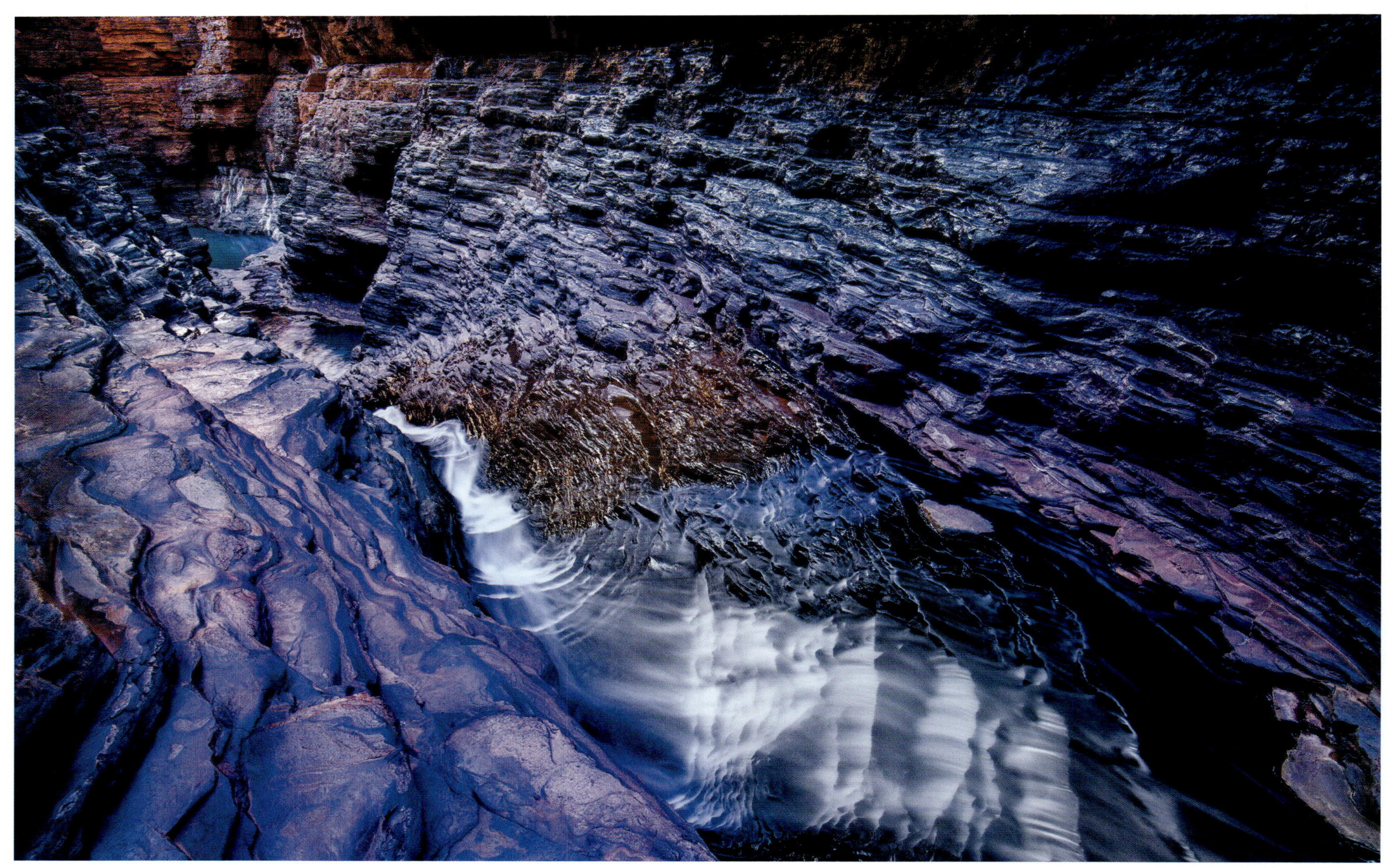

This is the classic Karijini photograph. At the end of Hancock Gorge the view of this little waterfall running in a tunnel of light is spectacular. Although I have enhanced the saturation and contrast of the photograph, I have tried to represent the color of the place as I felt it.

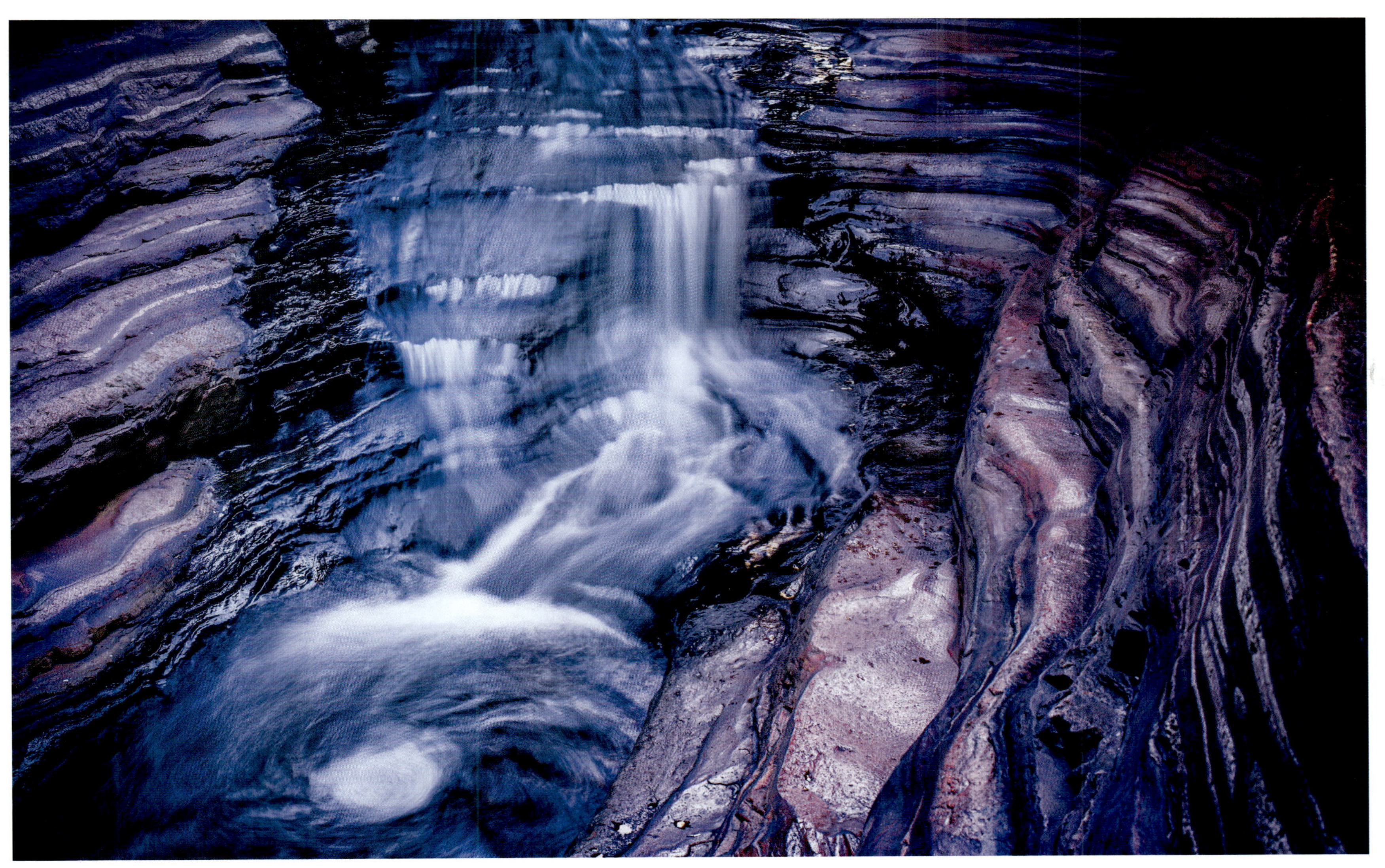

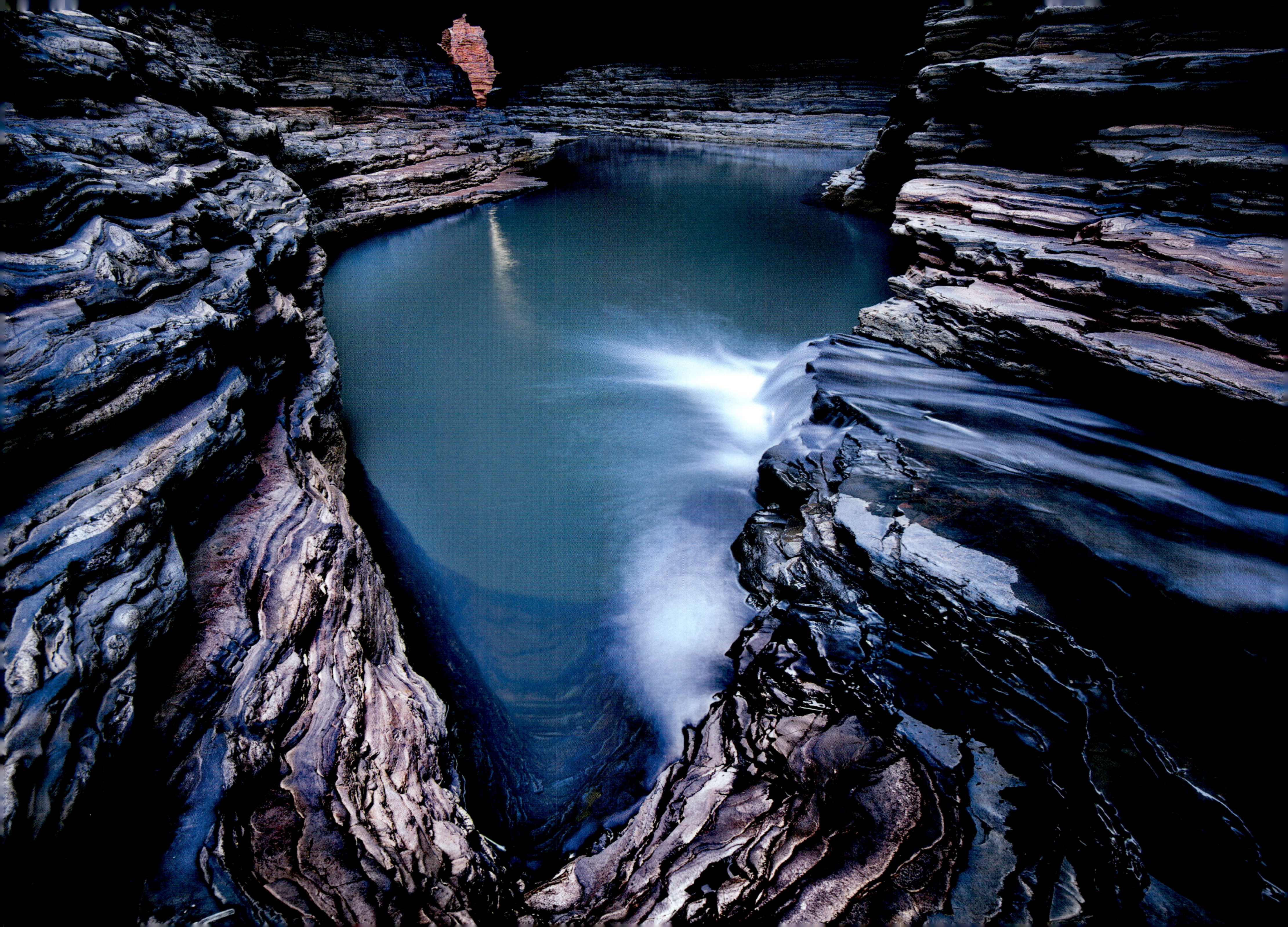

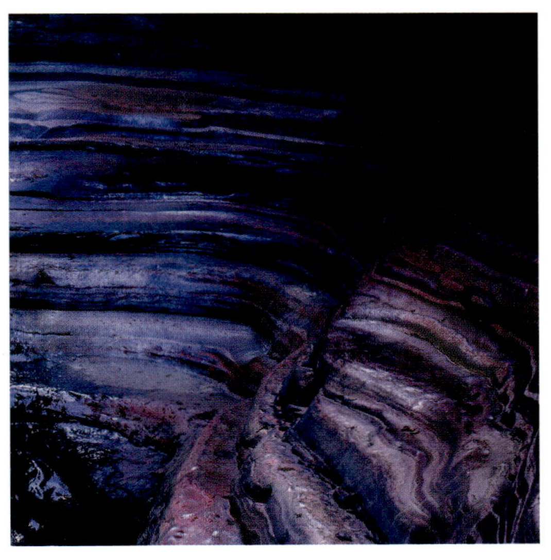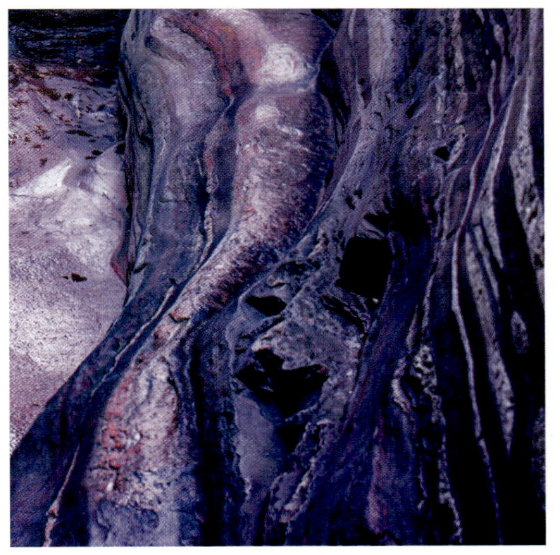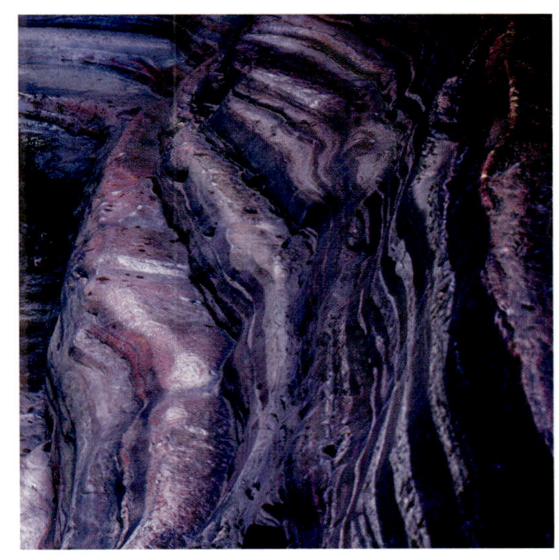

The walk into the depths of this gorge was challenging but one of the most fascinating ones I have done in Australia. There was climbing and swimming involved among narrow tunnels of rock along subterranean waterways. The effort was well rewarded with magnificent pictures.

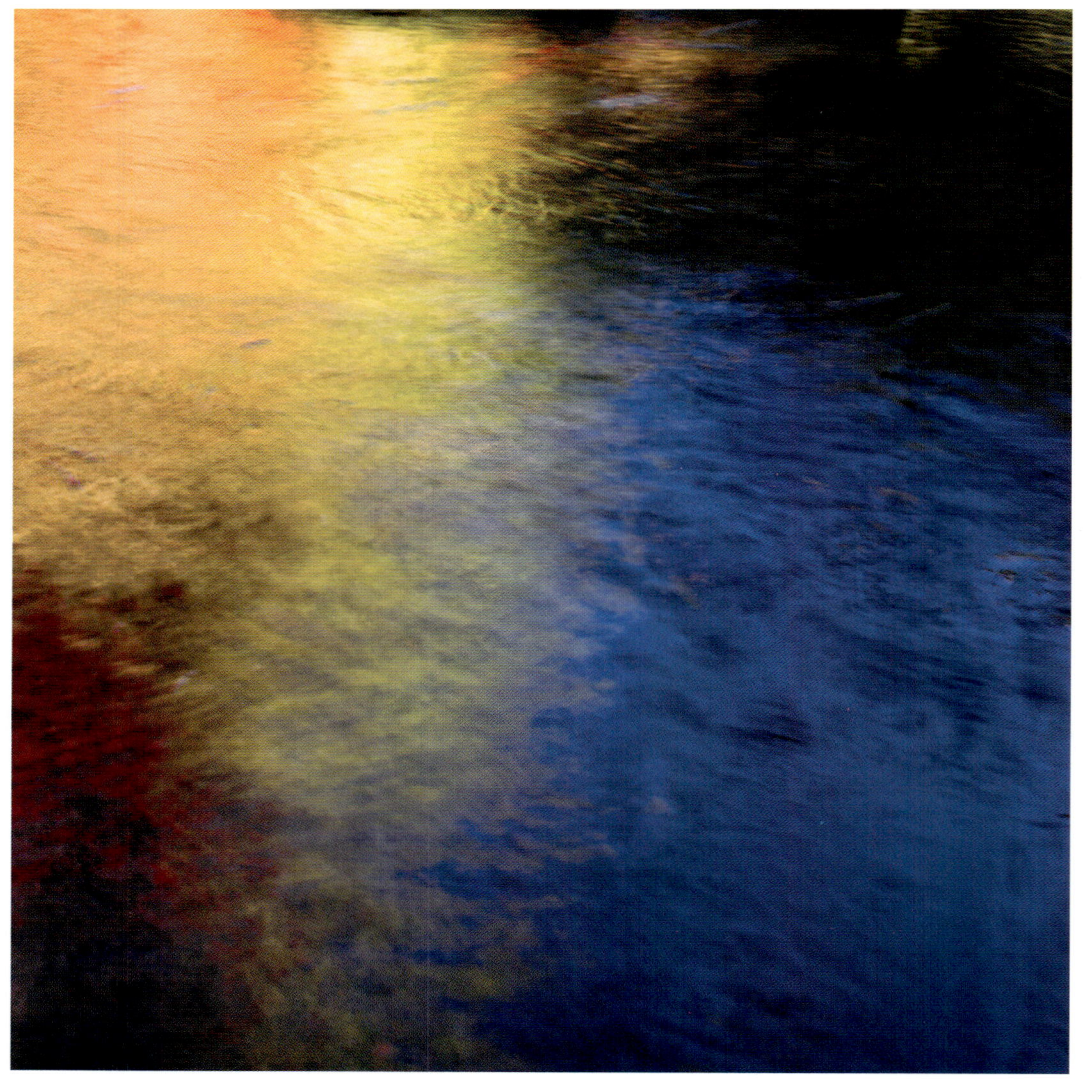

KALAMINA GORGE

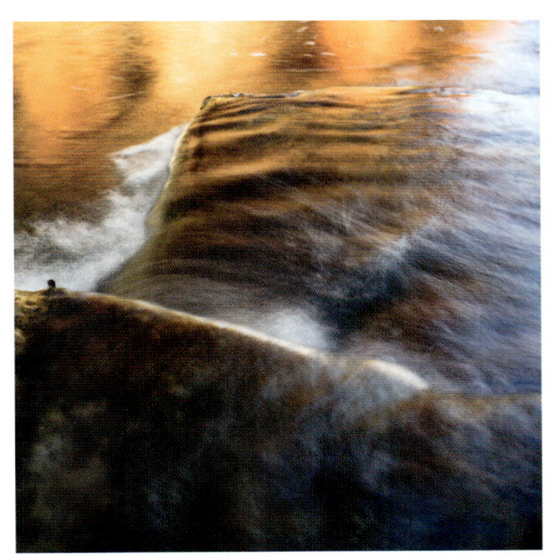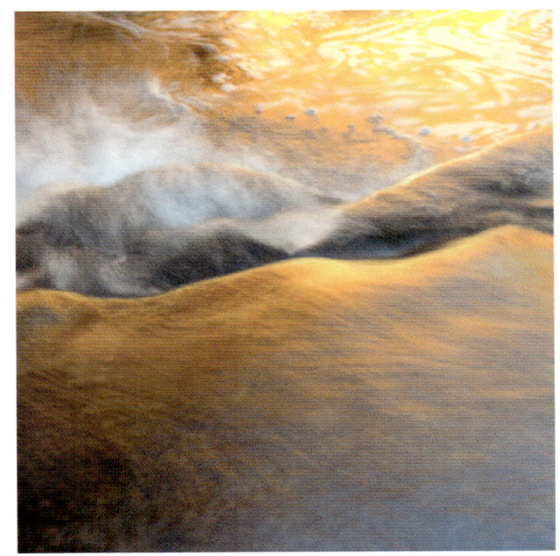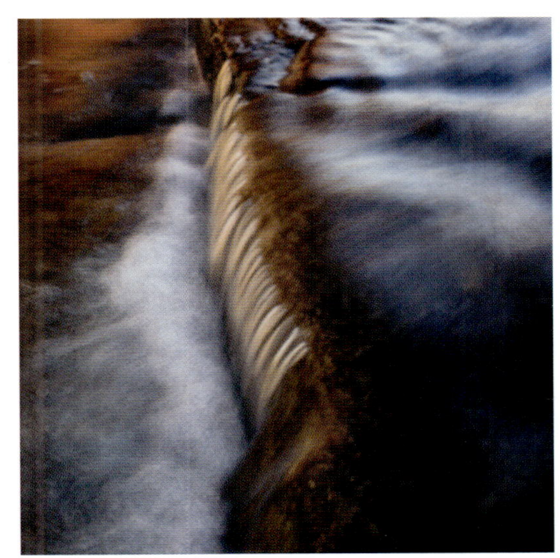

Kalamina Falls is a seasonal waterfall sitting at the head of the Kalamina Gorge. The reflections on the water during sunrise and sunset are spectacular.

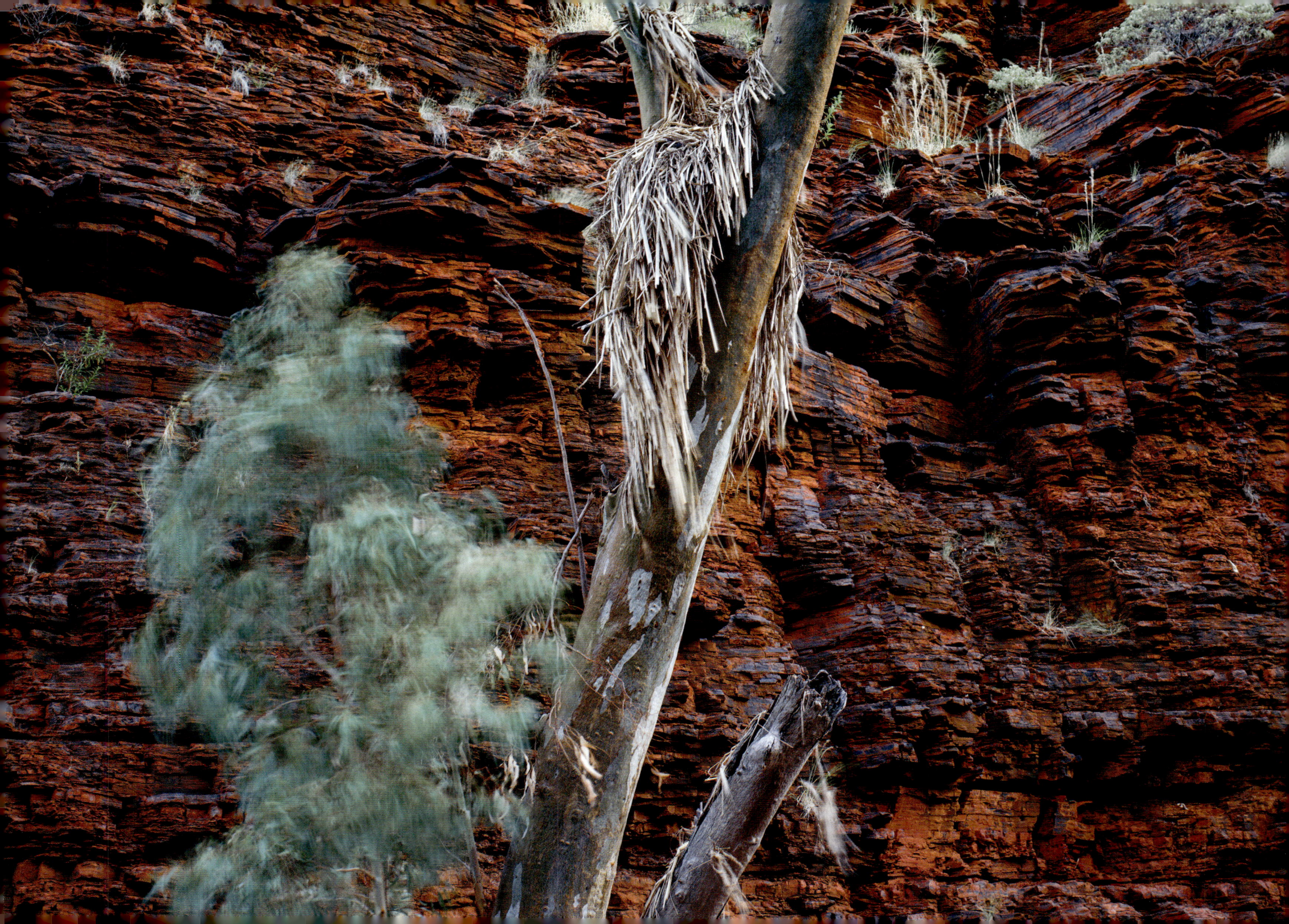

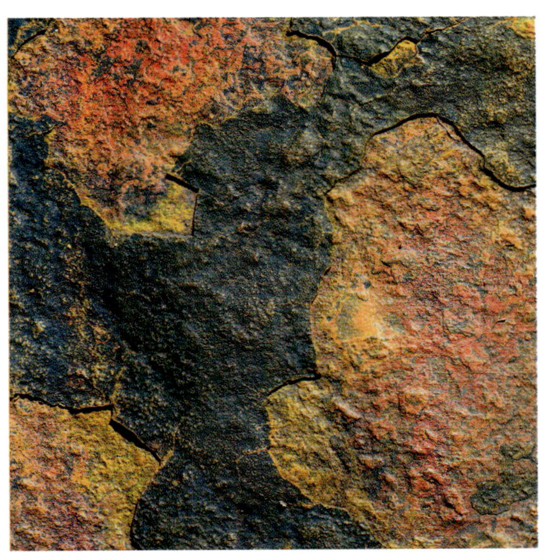 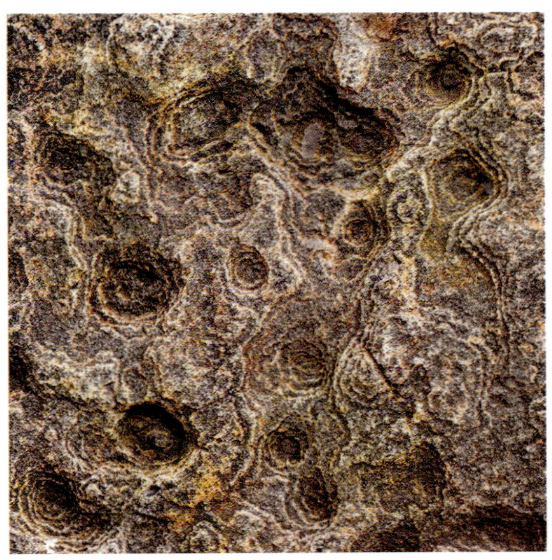 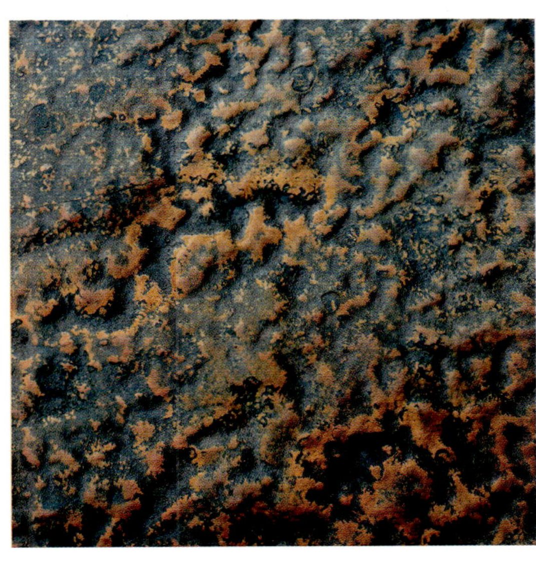

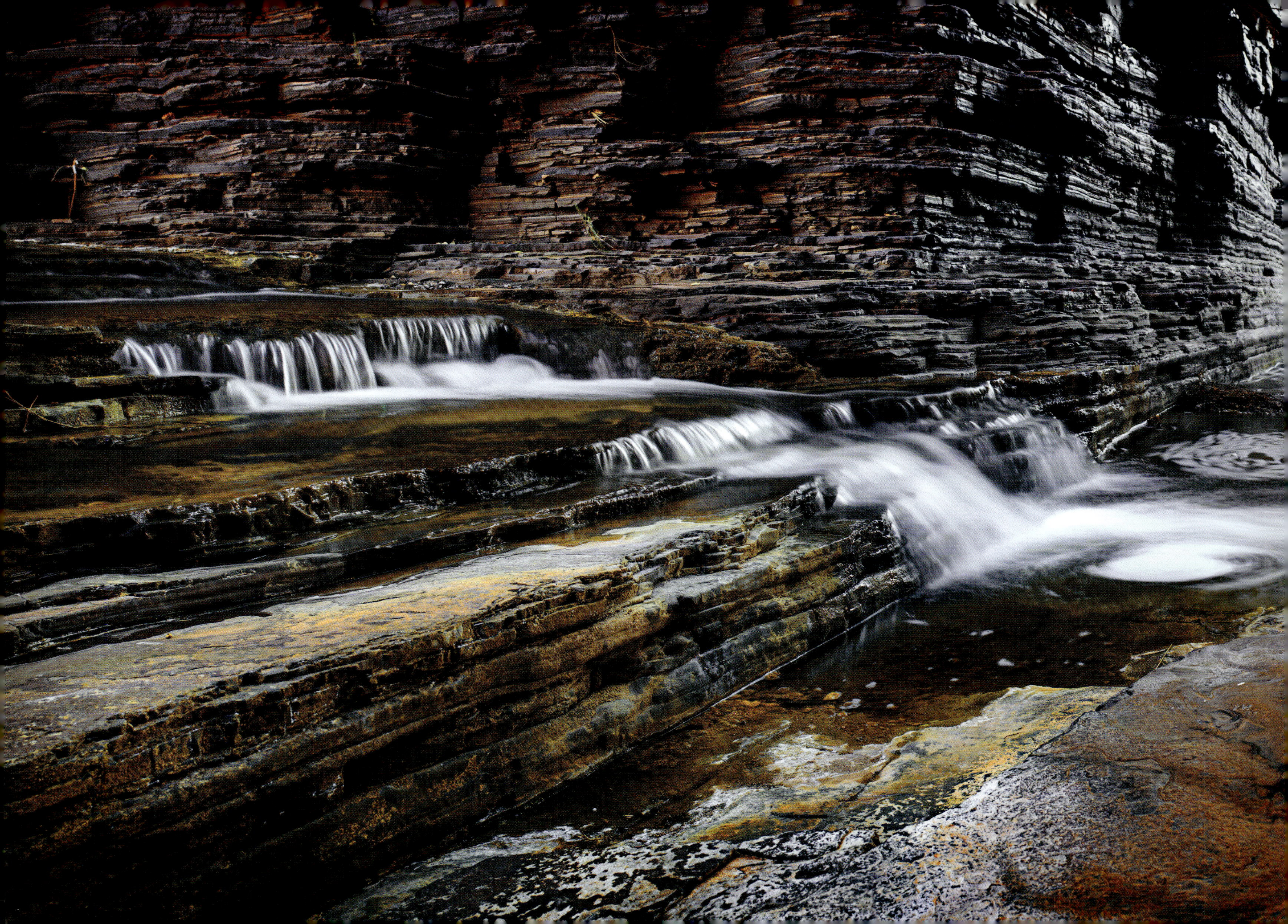

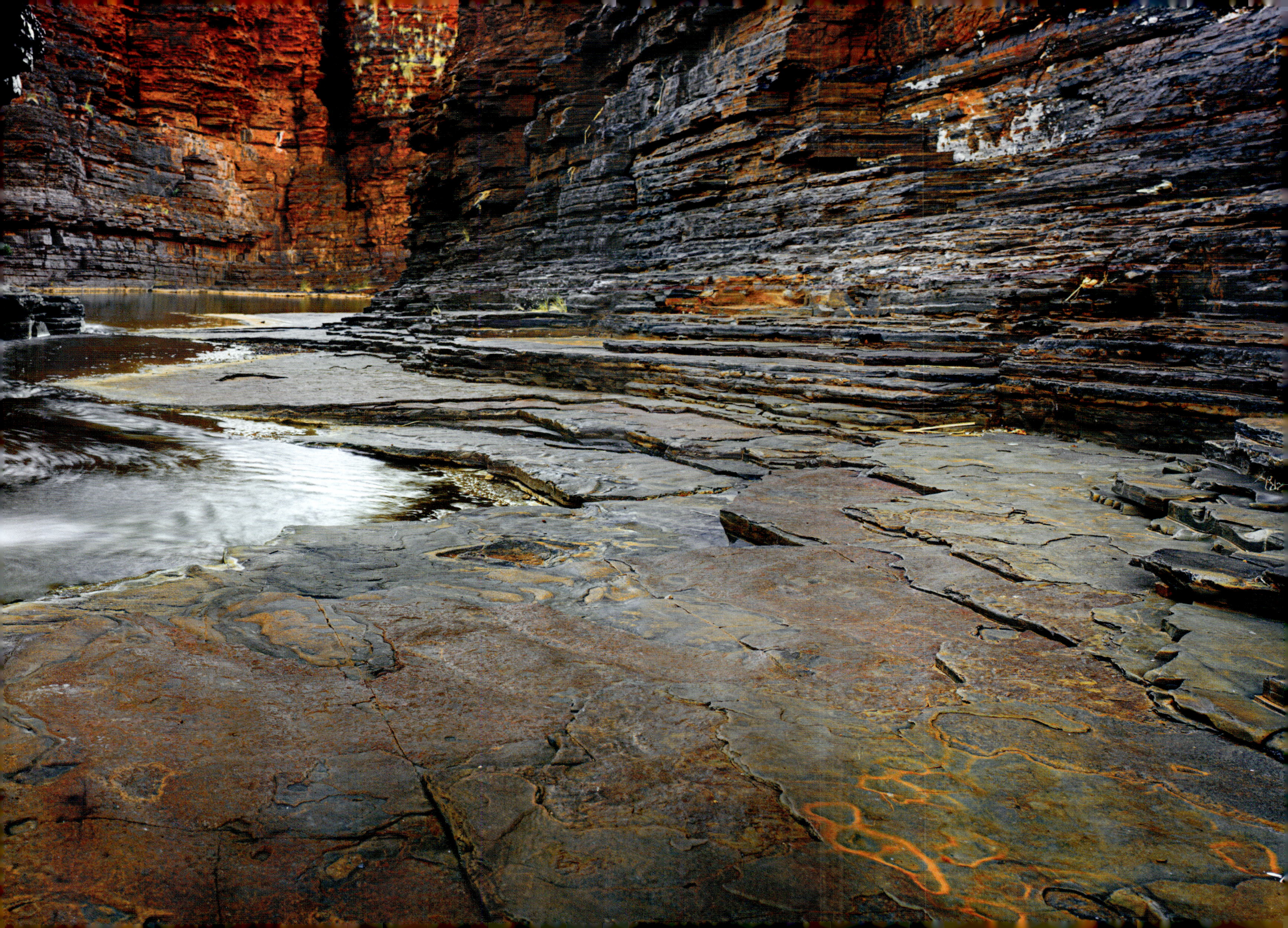

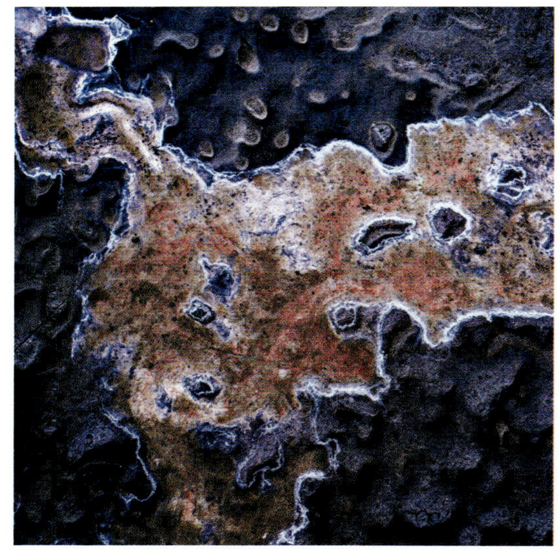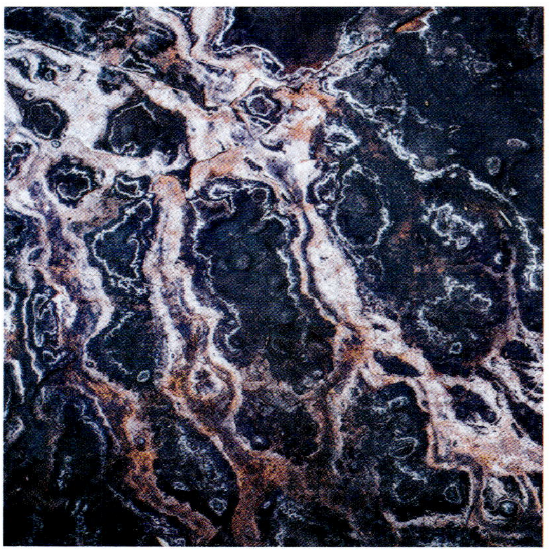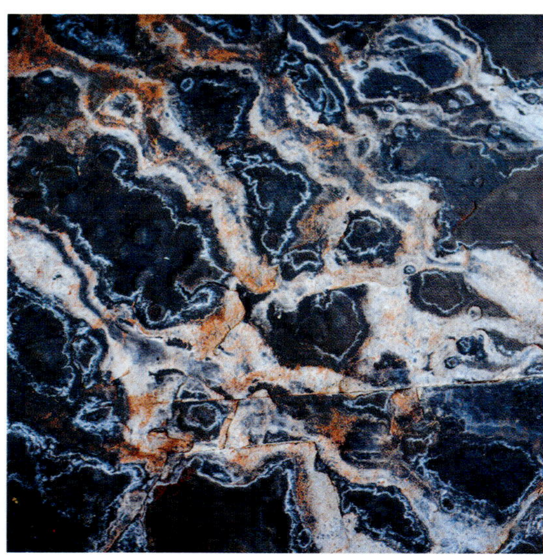

   KALAMINA GORGE

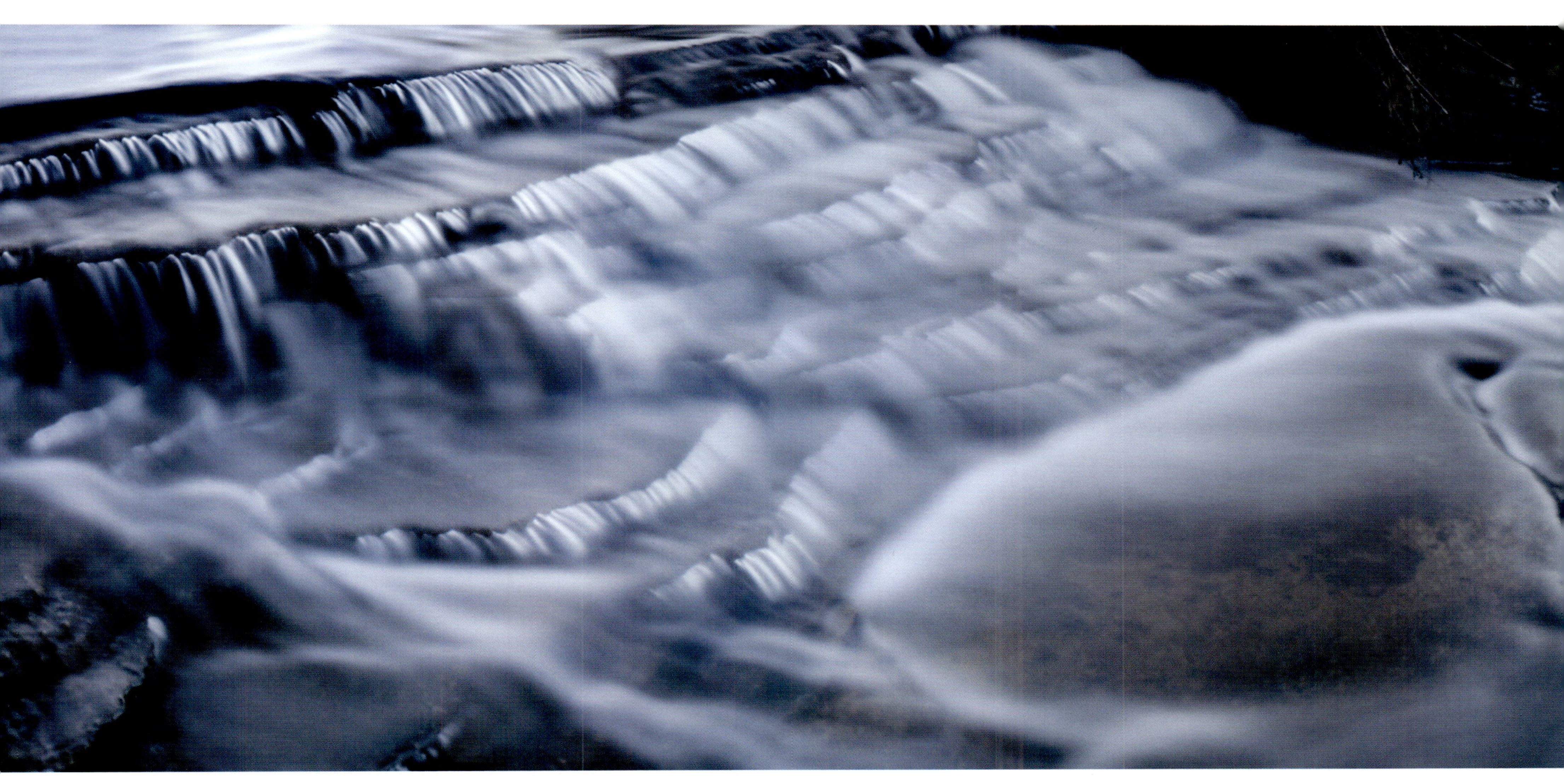

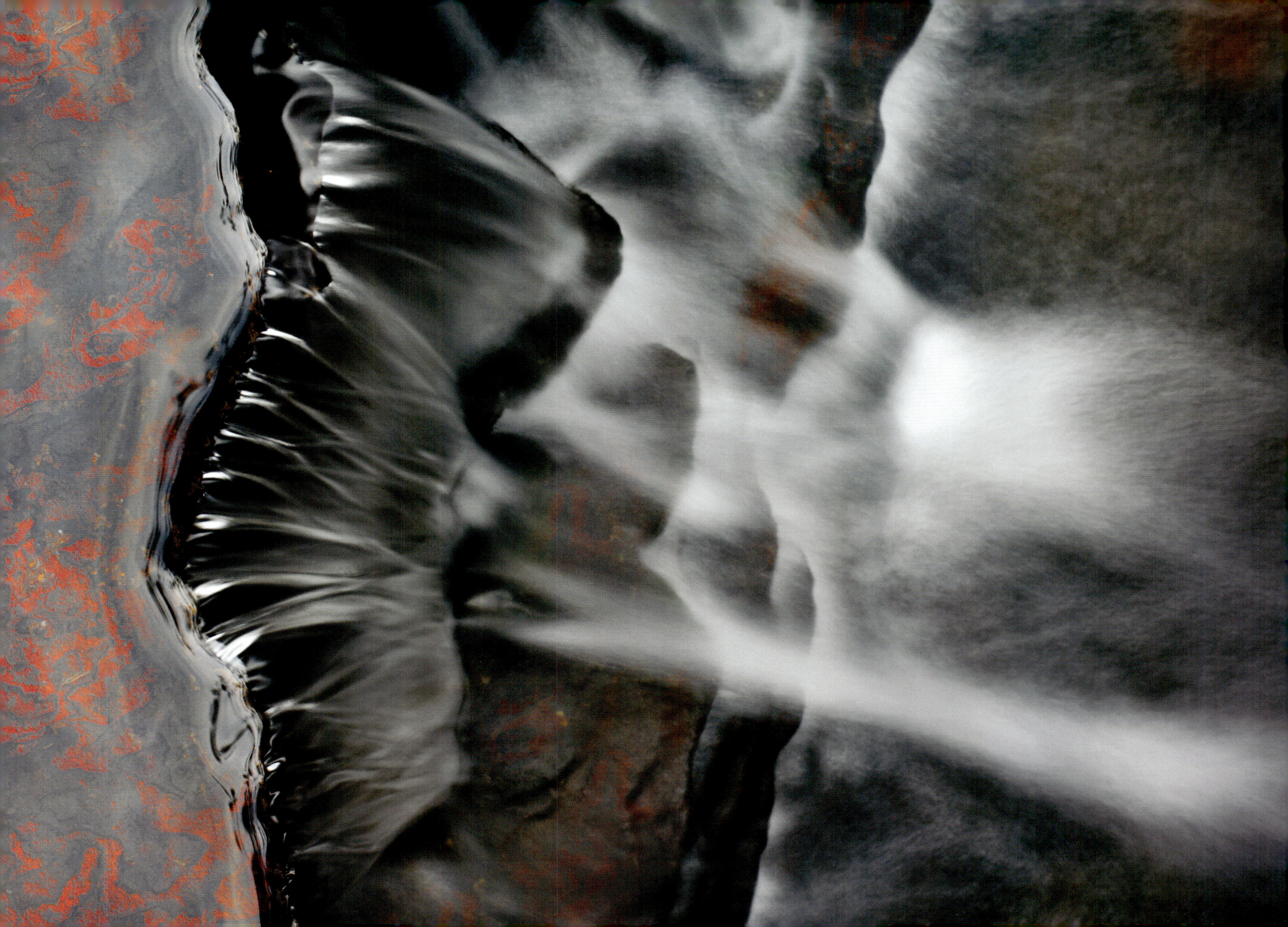

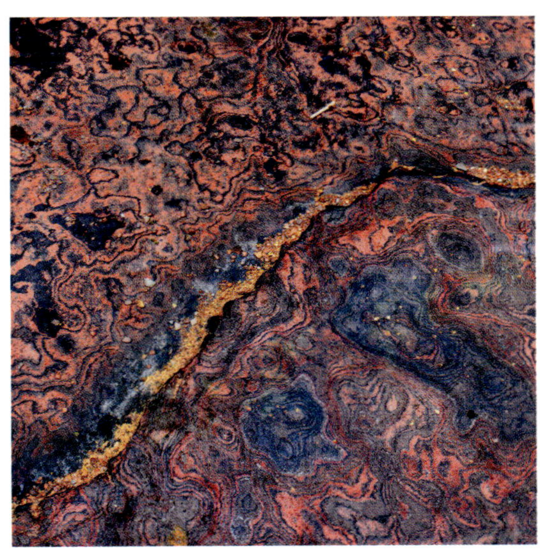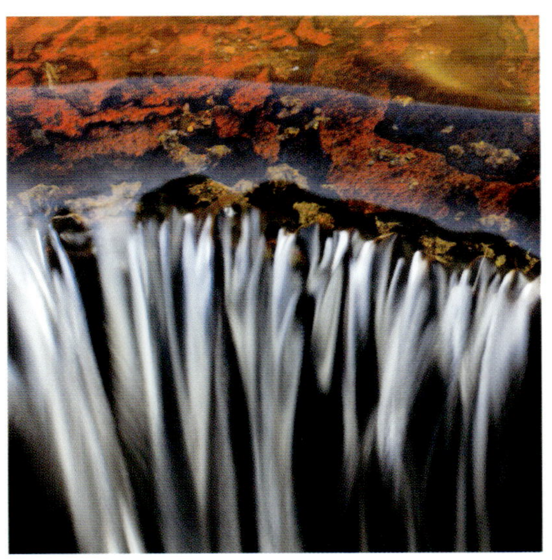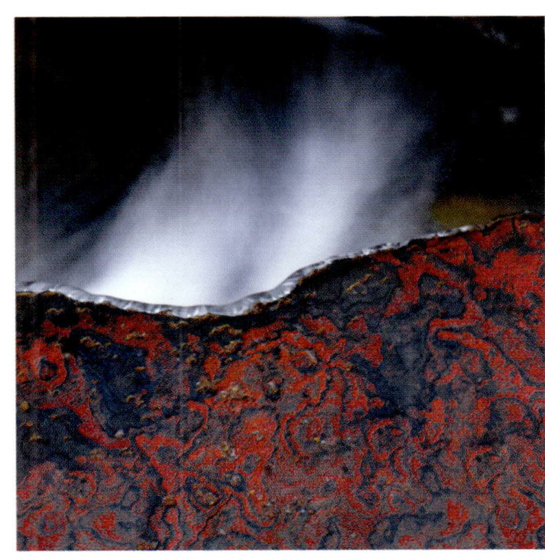

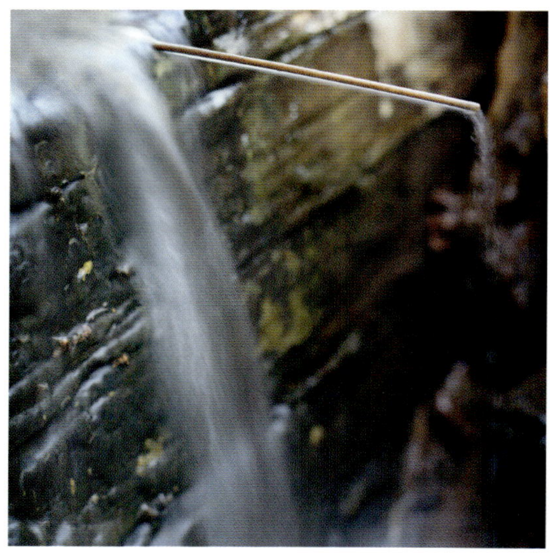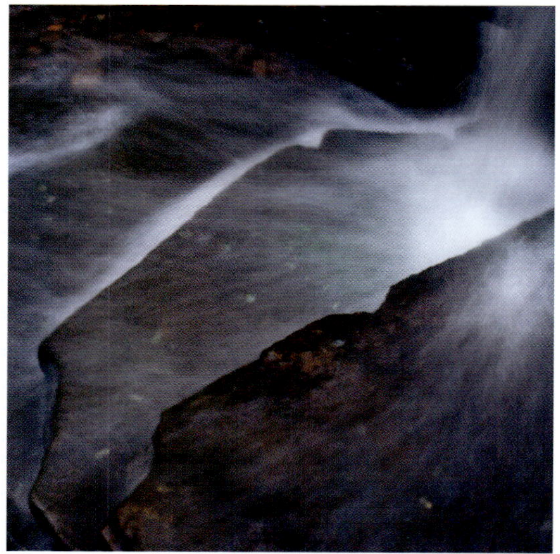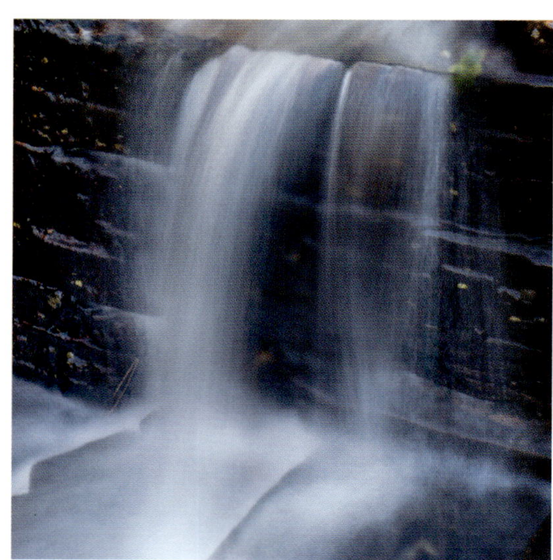

  KNOX GORGE

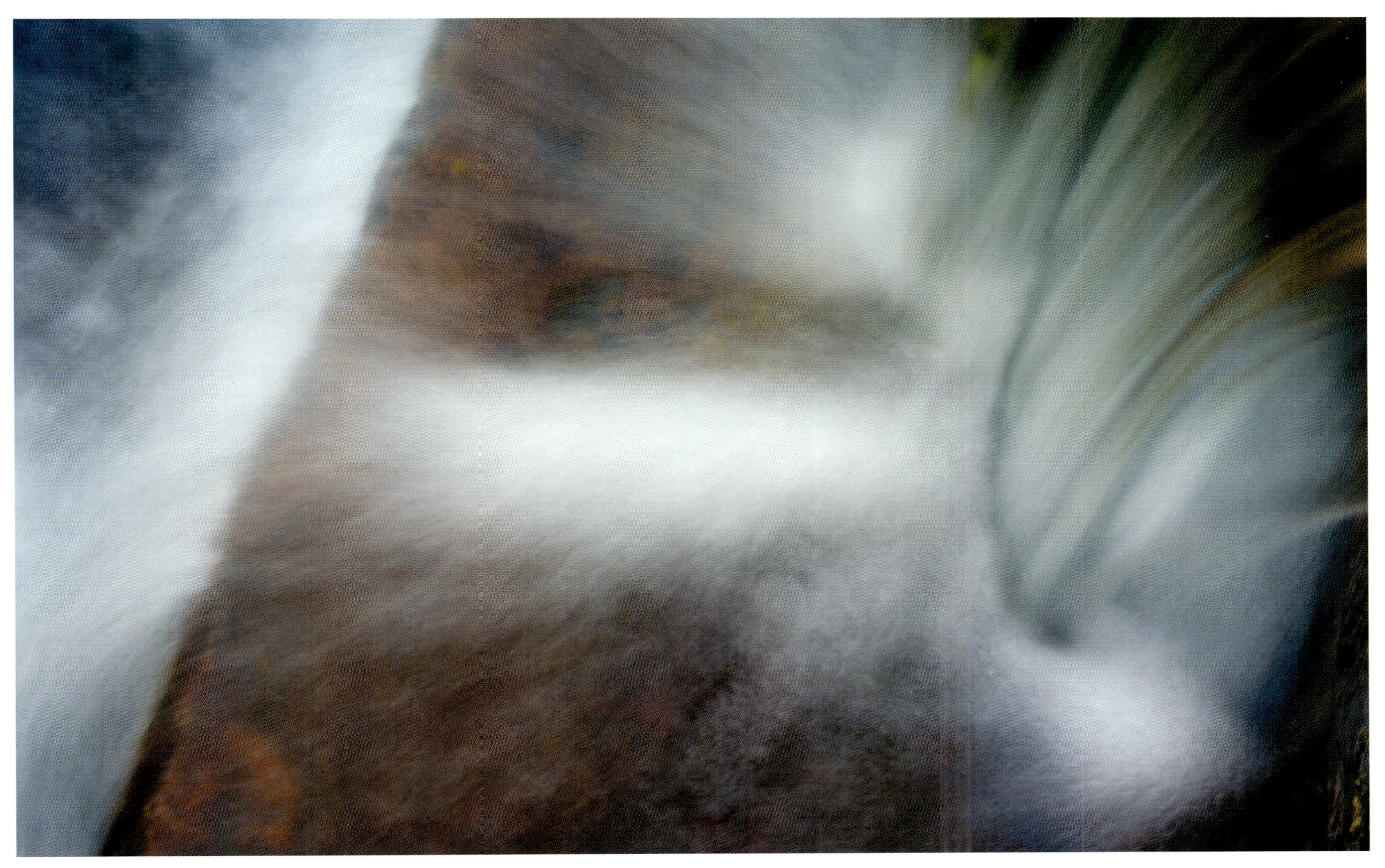

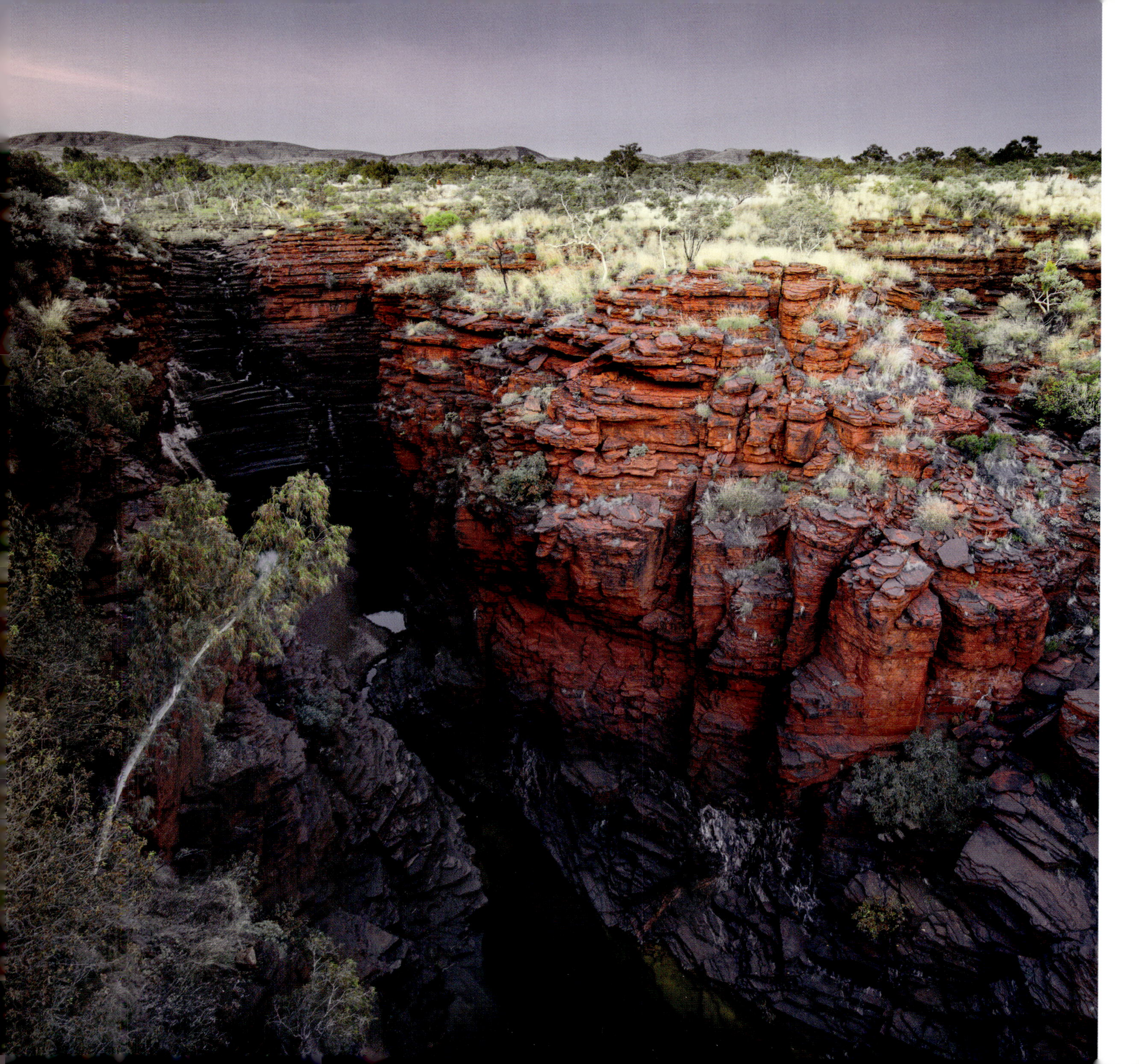

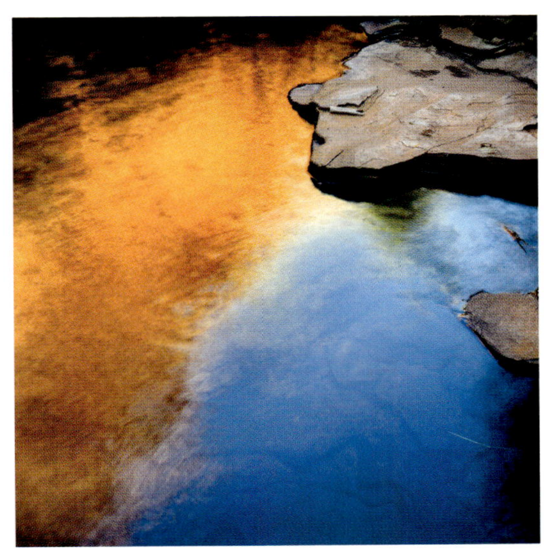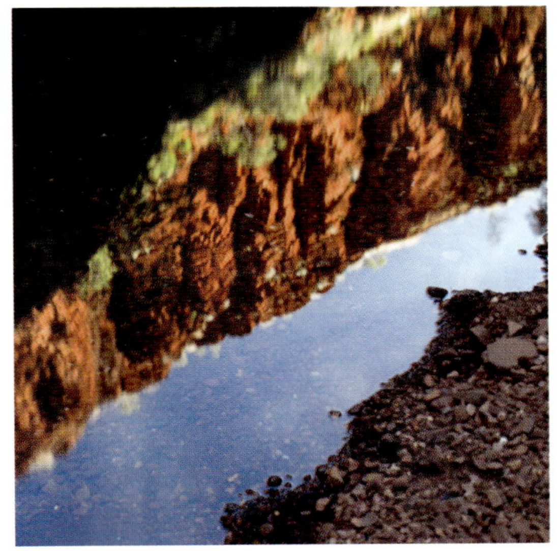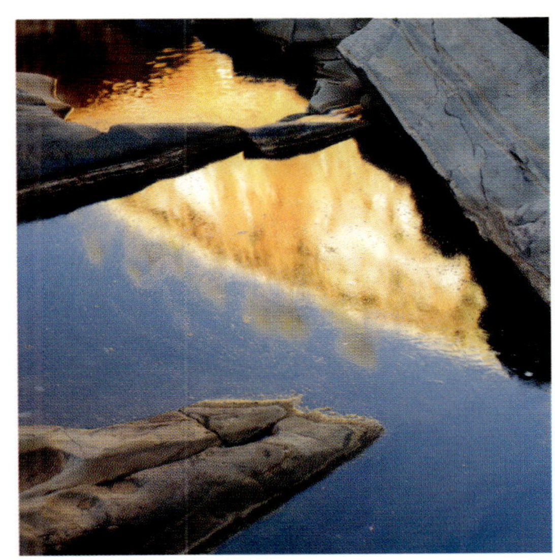

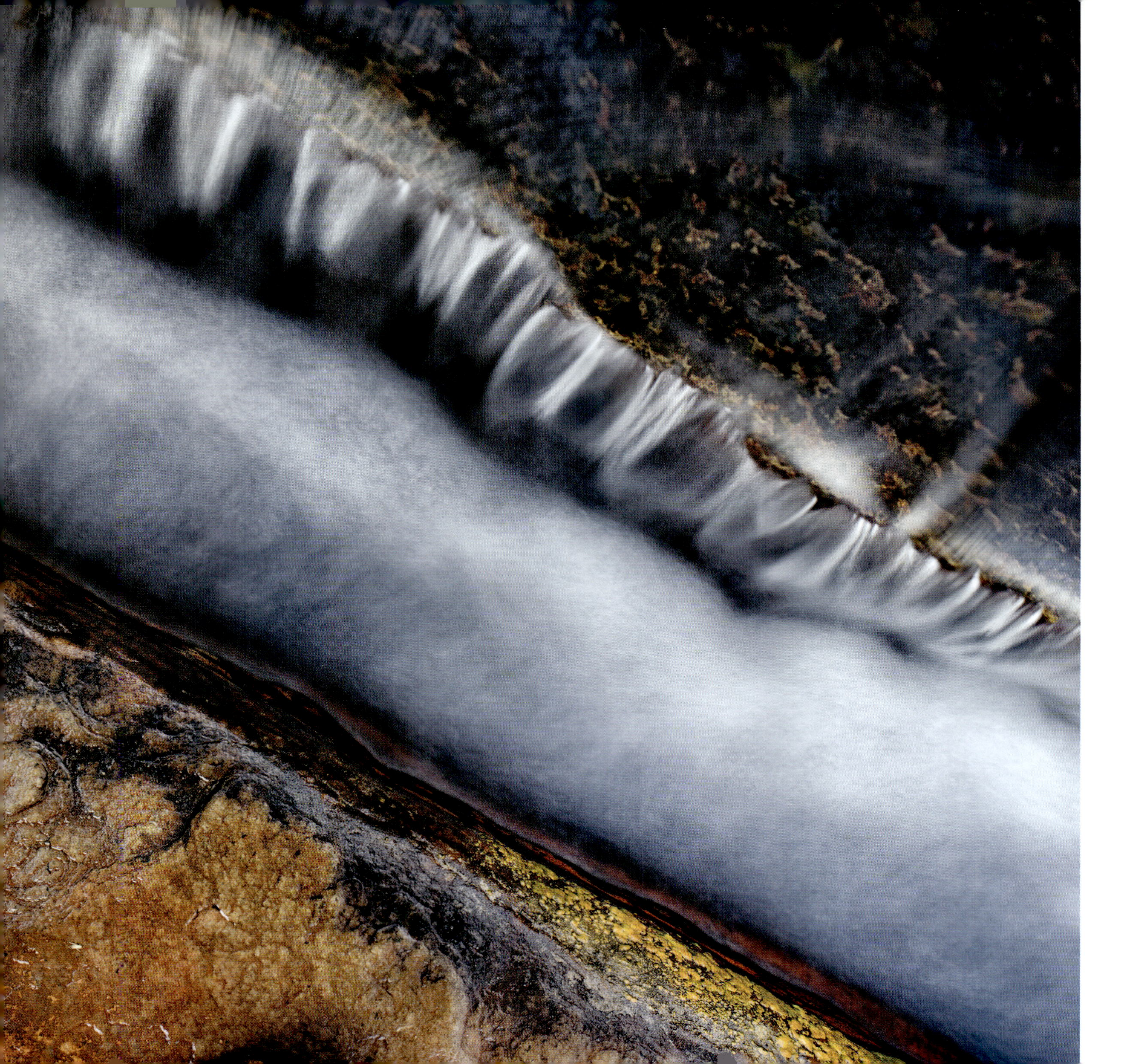

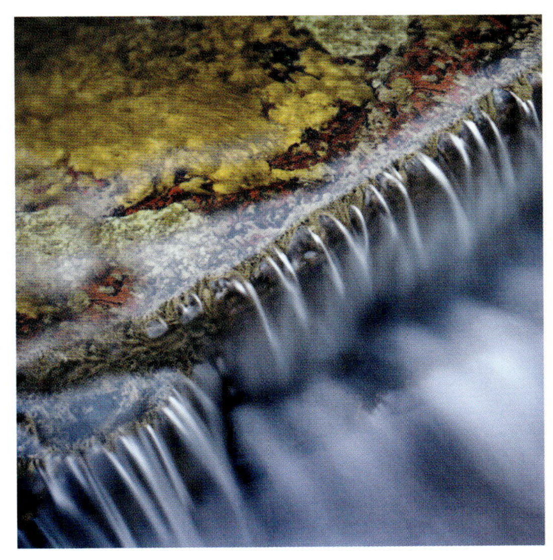 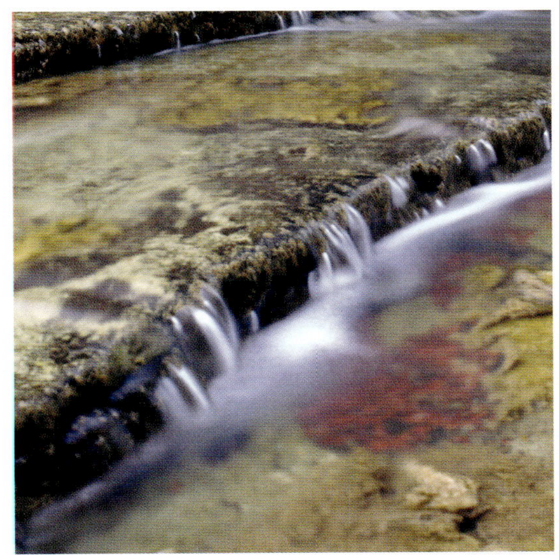 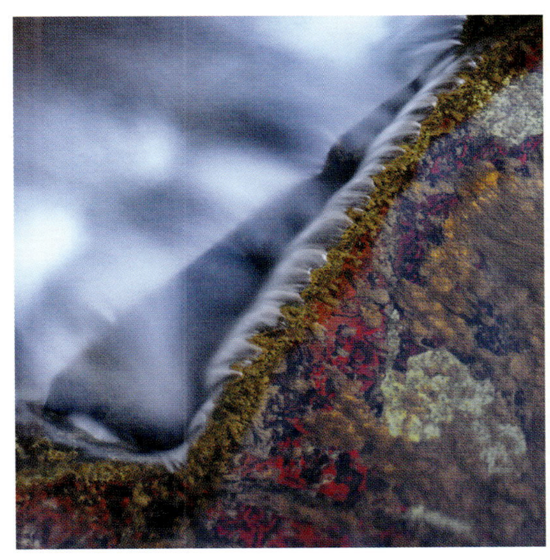

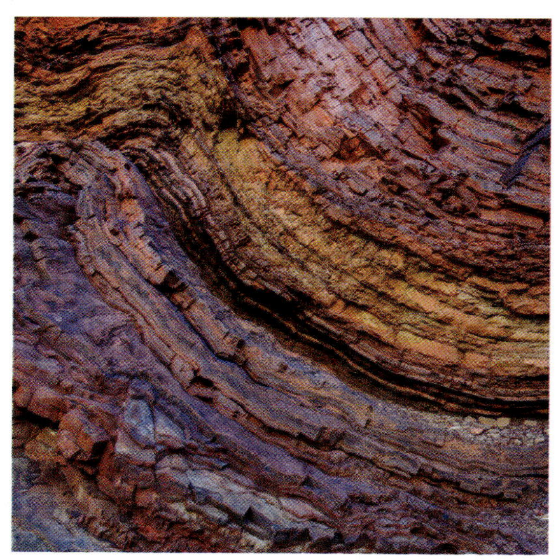 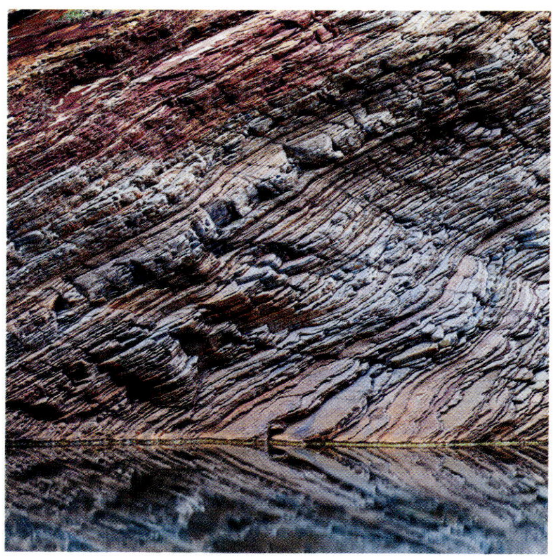 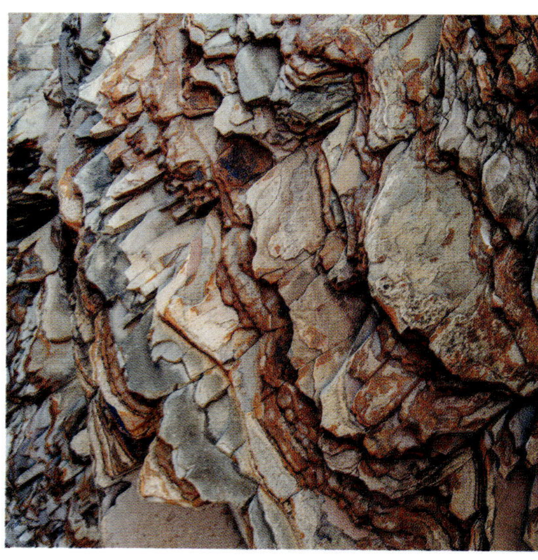

Hamersley Gorge

(Opposite page) This photograph was taken using a photographic technique called focus stacking. Focus stacking is a digital image processing technique which combines multiple images taken at different focal distances to give a resulting image with a greater depth of field. This way the image appears to be in focus all the way from the foreground to the background.

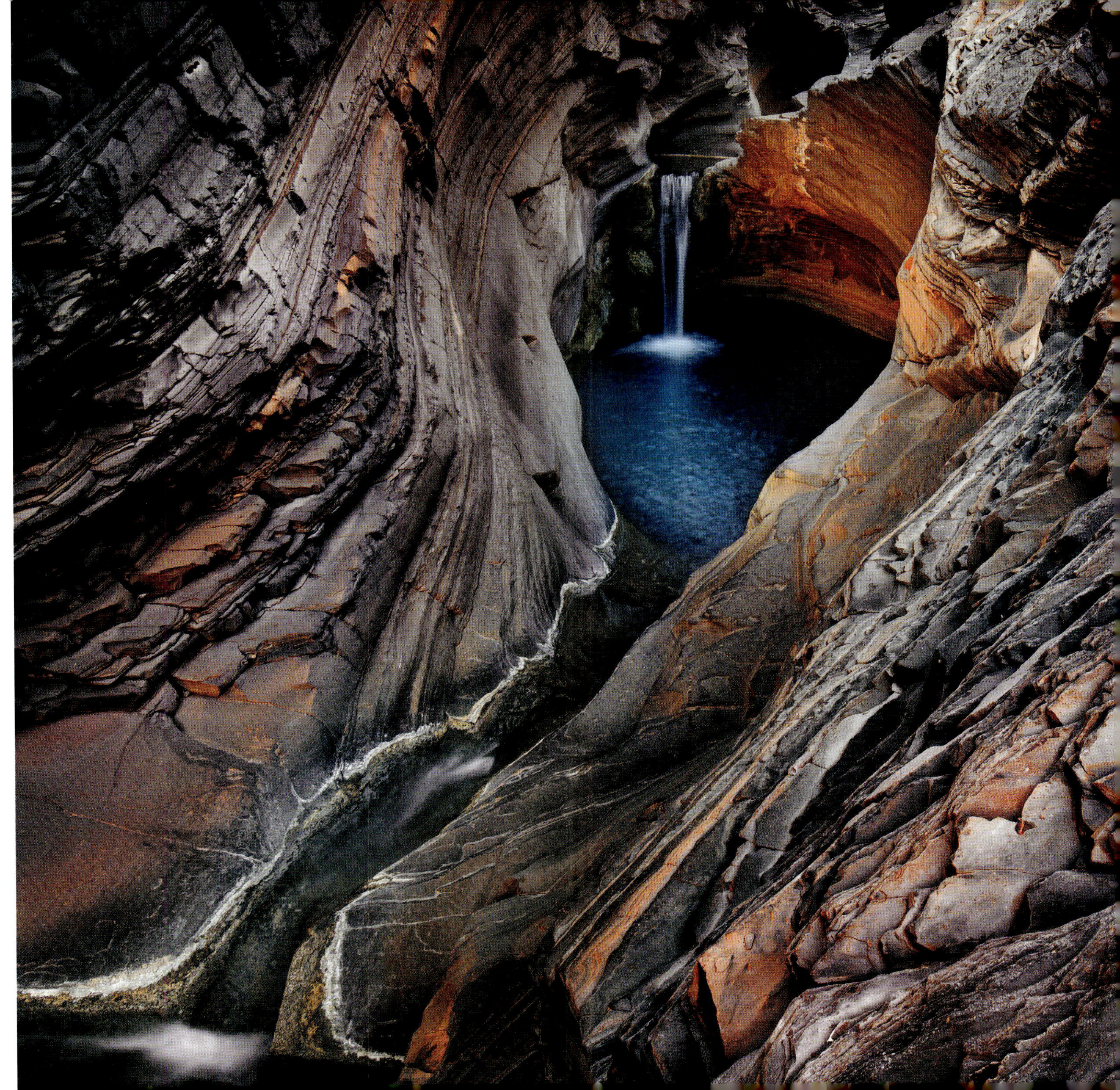

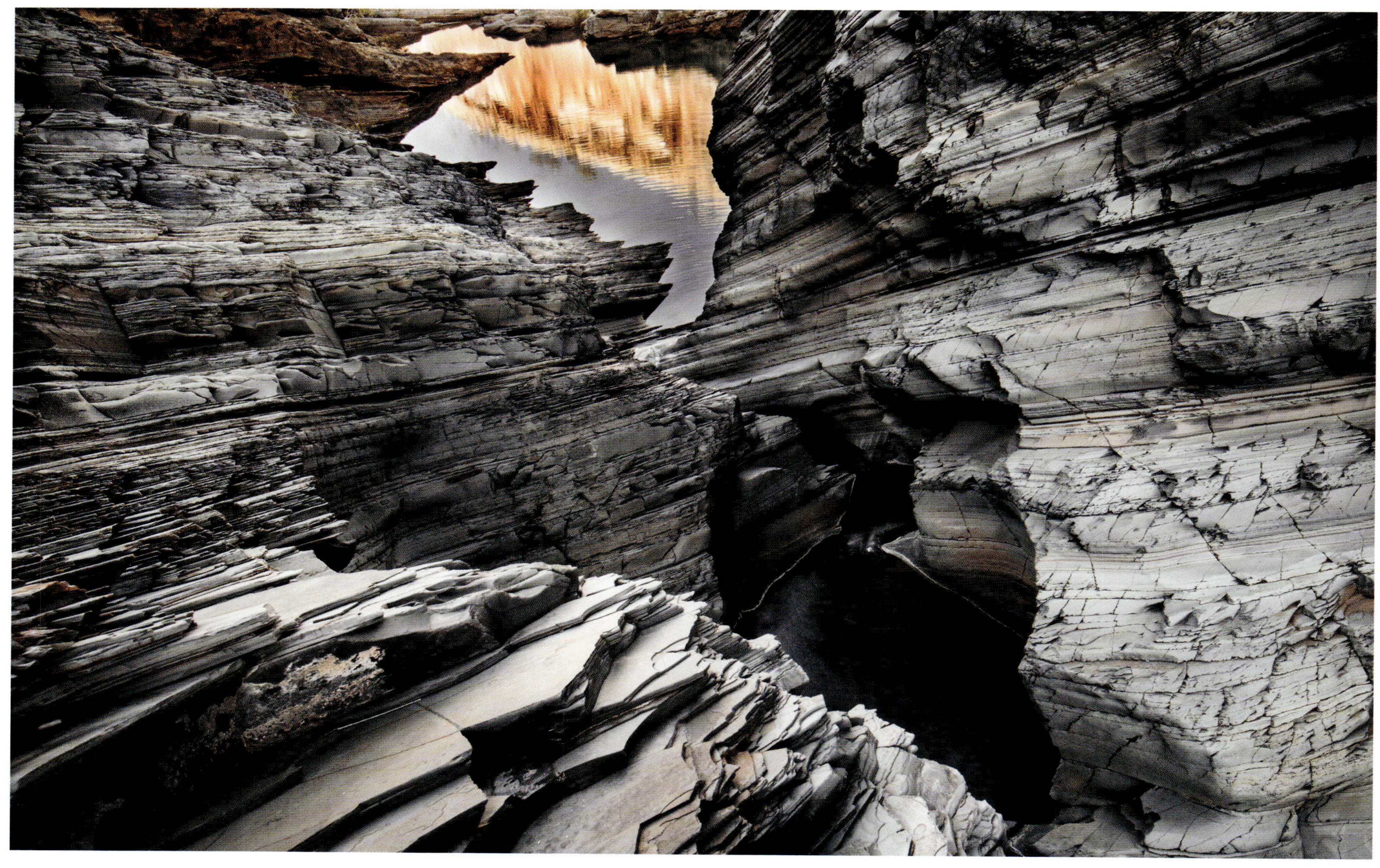

HAMERSLEY GORGE

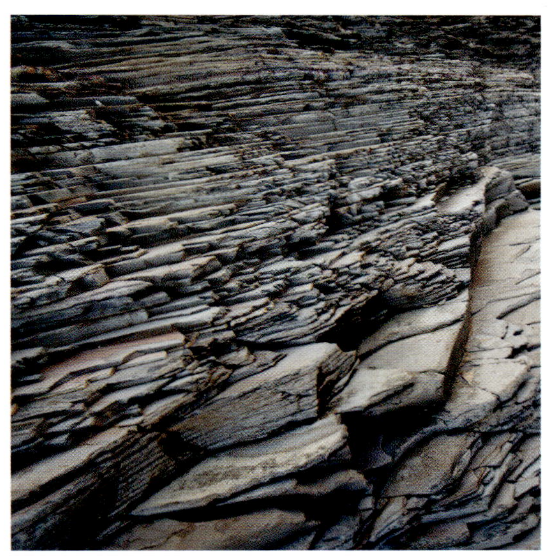 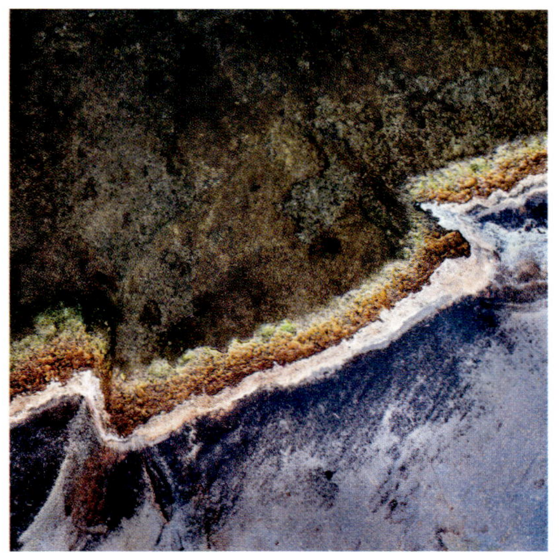 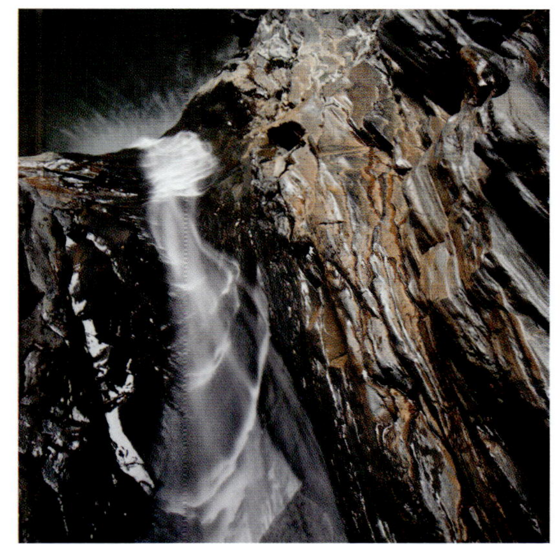

Hamersley is a very different type of gorge to the rest of the gorges in Karijin . It has dramatic colours, textures and reflections and a beautiful waterfall to complete the brilliant scenery. The pictures around Hamersley gorge were taken during sunset.

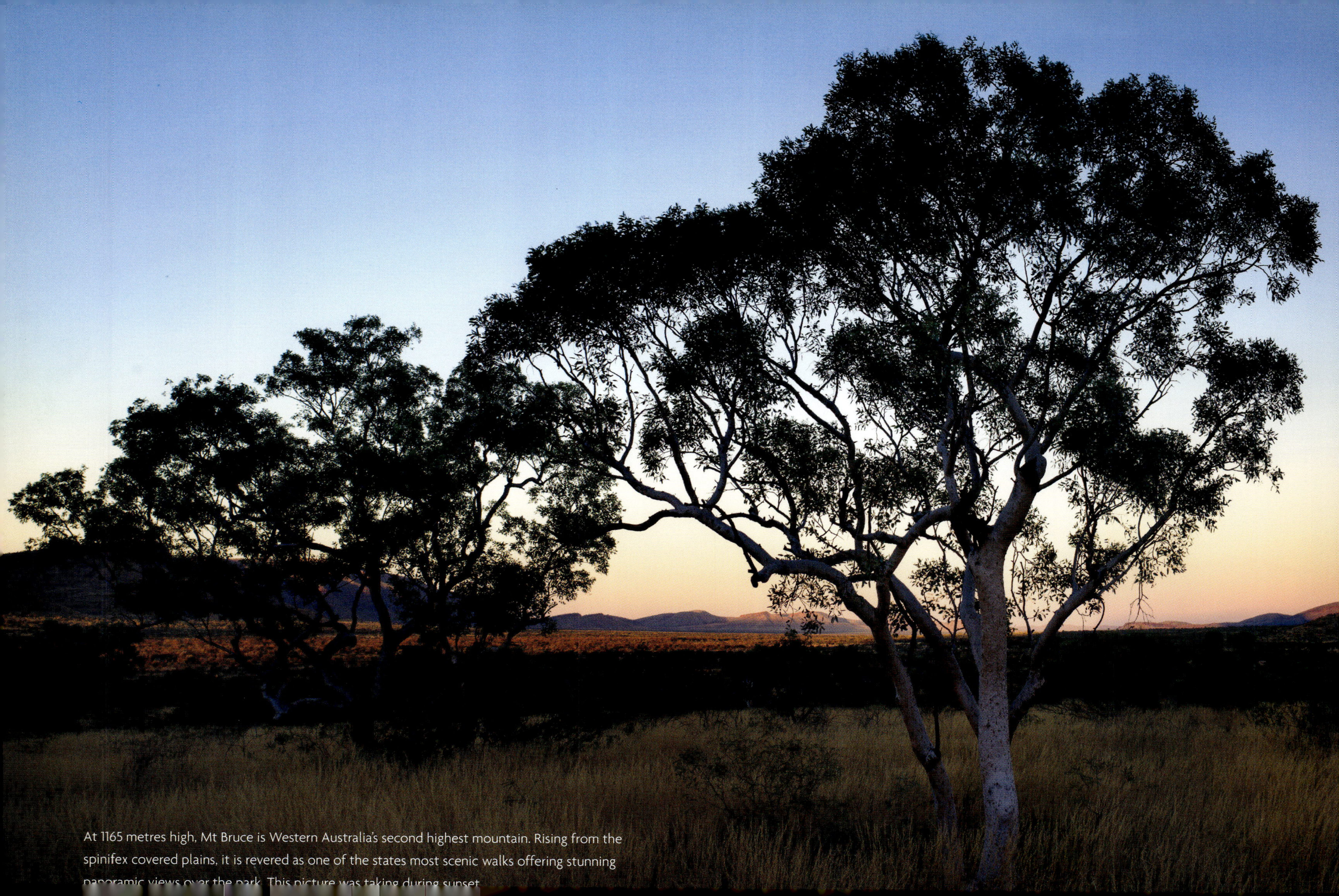

At 1165 metres high, Mt Bruce is Western Australia's second highest mountain. Rising from the spinifex covered plains, it is revered as one of the states most scenic walks offering stunning panoramic views over the park. This picture was taking during sunset.

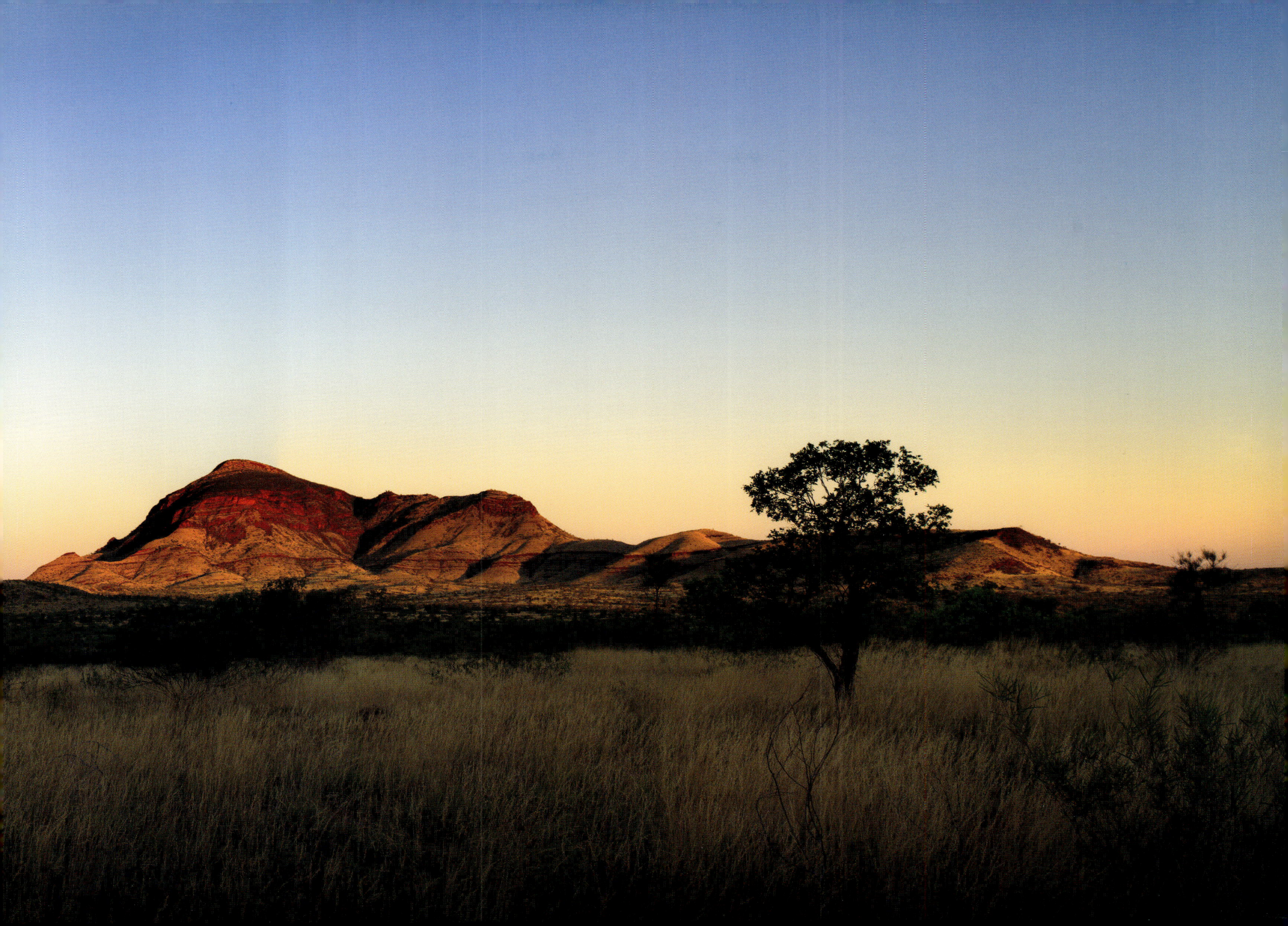

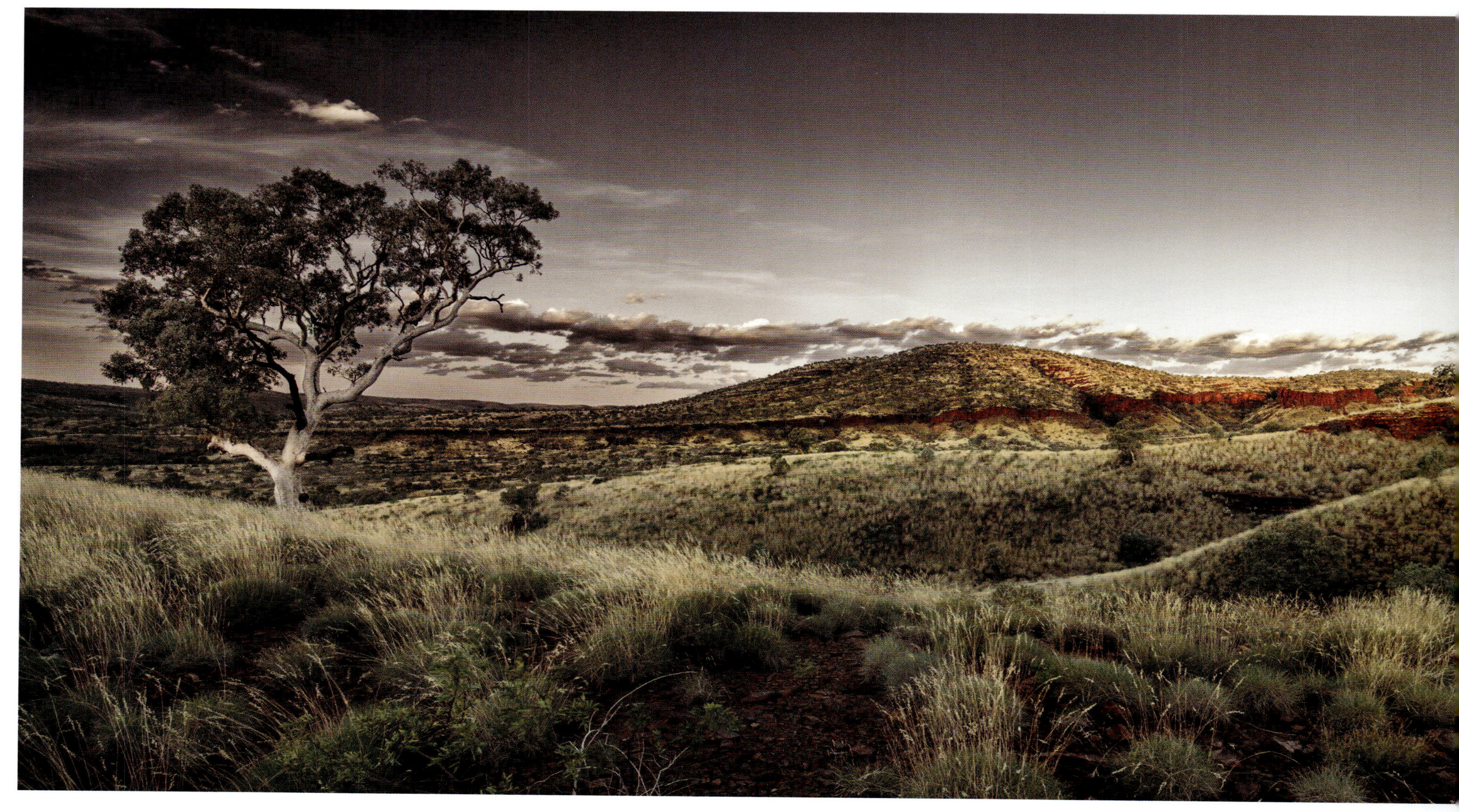

KARIJINI NATIONAL PARK

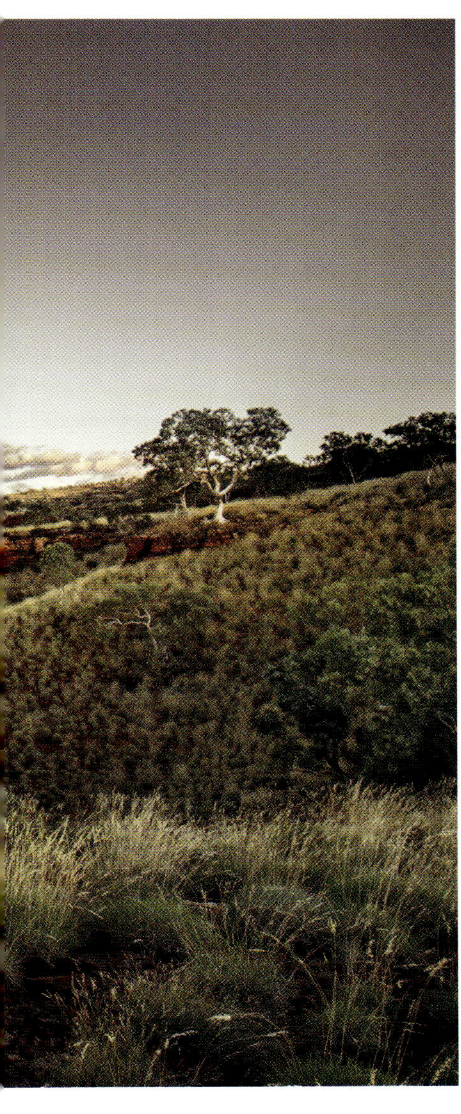

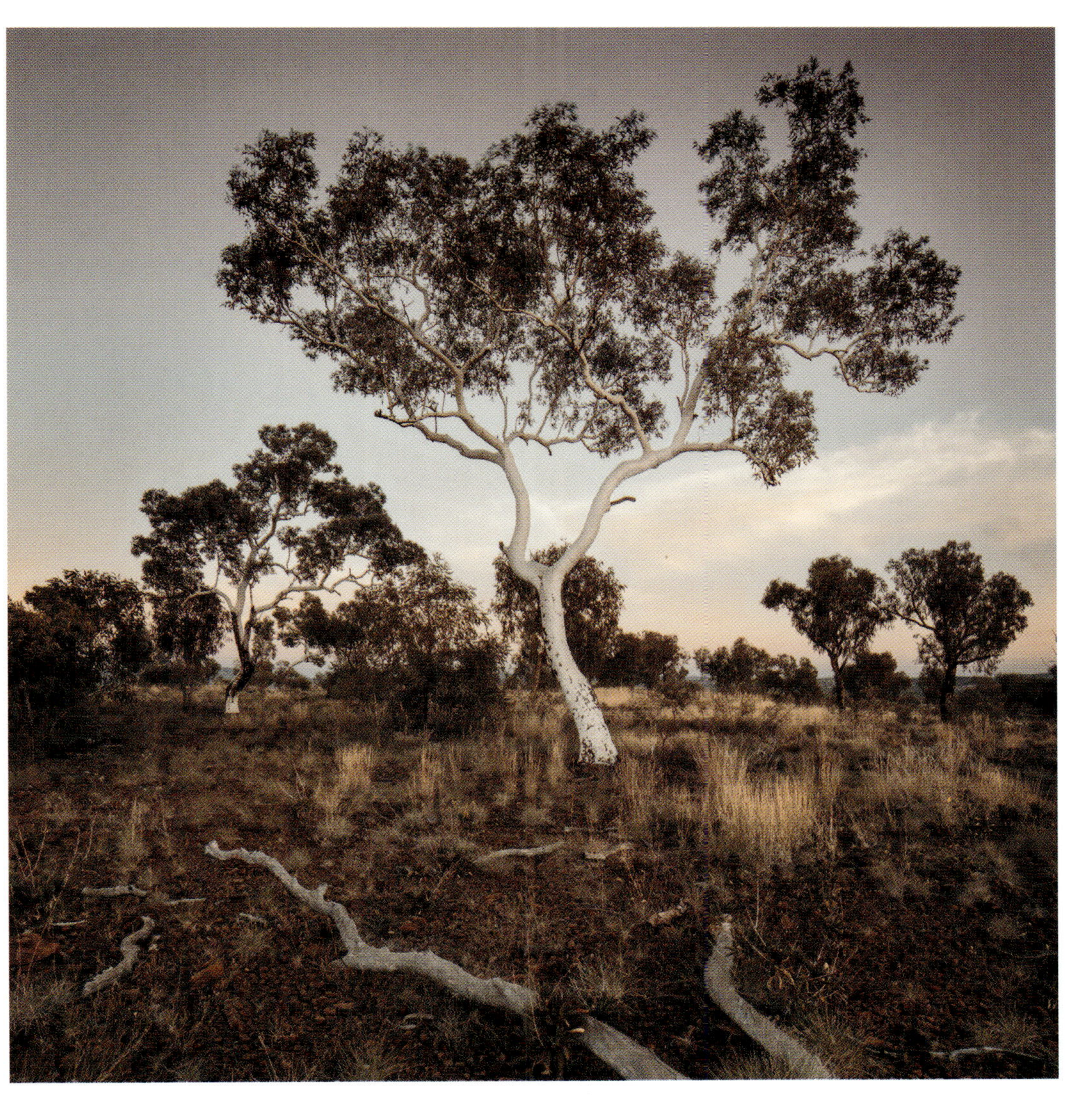

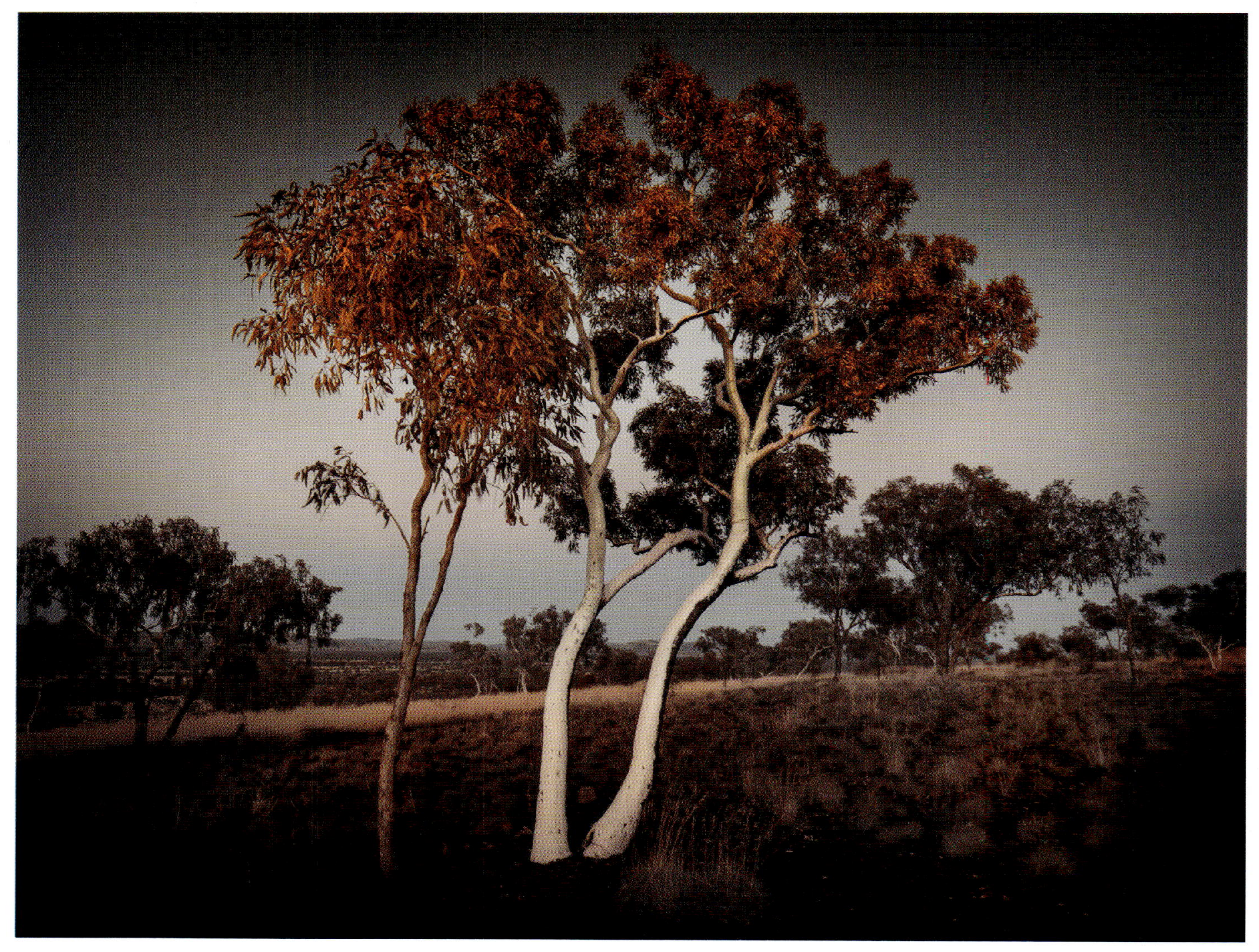

   KARIJINI NATIONAL PARK

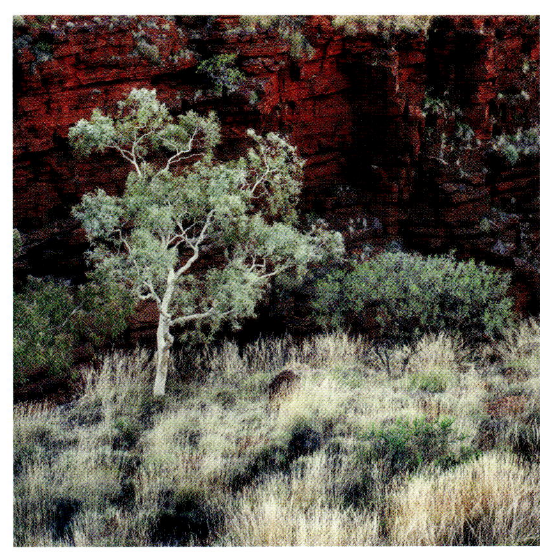 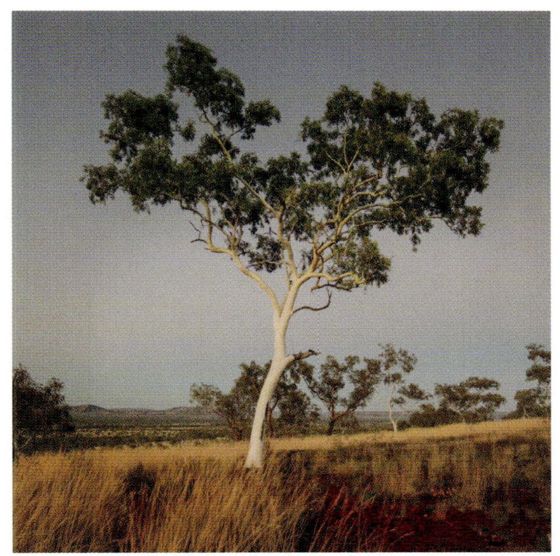 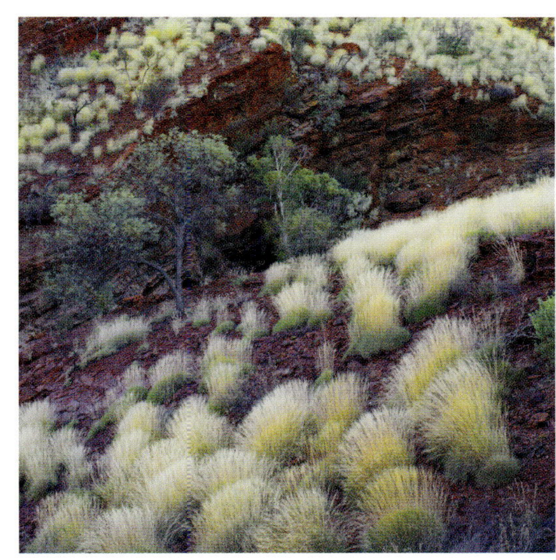

The Australian Eucalyptus tree is the most classic Australian tree. It's a huge genus that consists of over 700 species, the vast majority of which are endemic to Australia. Many are known as gum trees because they exude copious sap from any break in the bark. The Australian Aborigines have used eucalyptus for hundreds of years as a remedy for fever, wounds, coughs and joint pain.

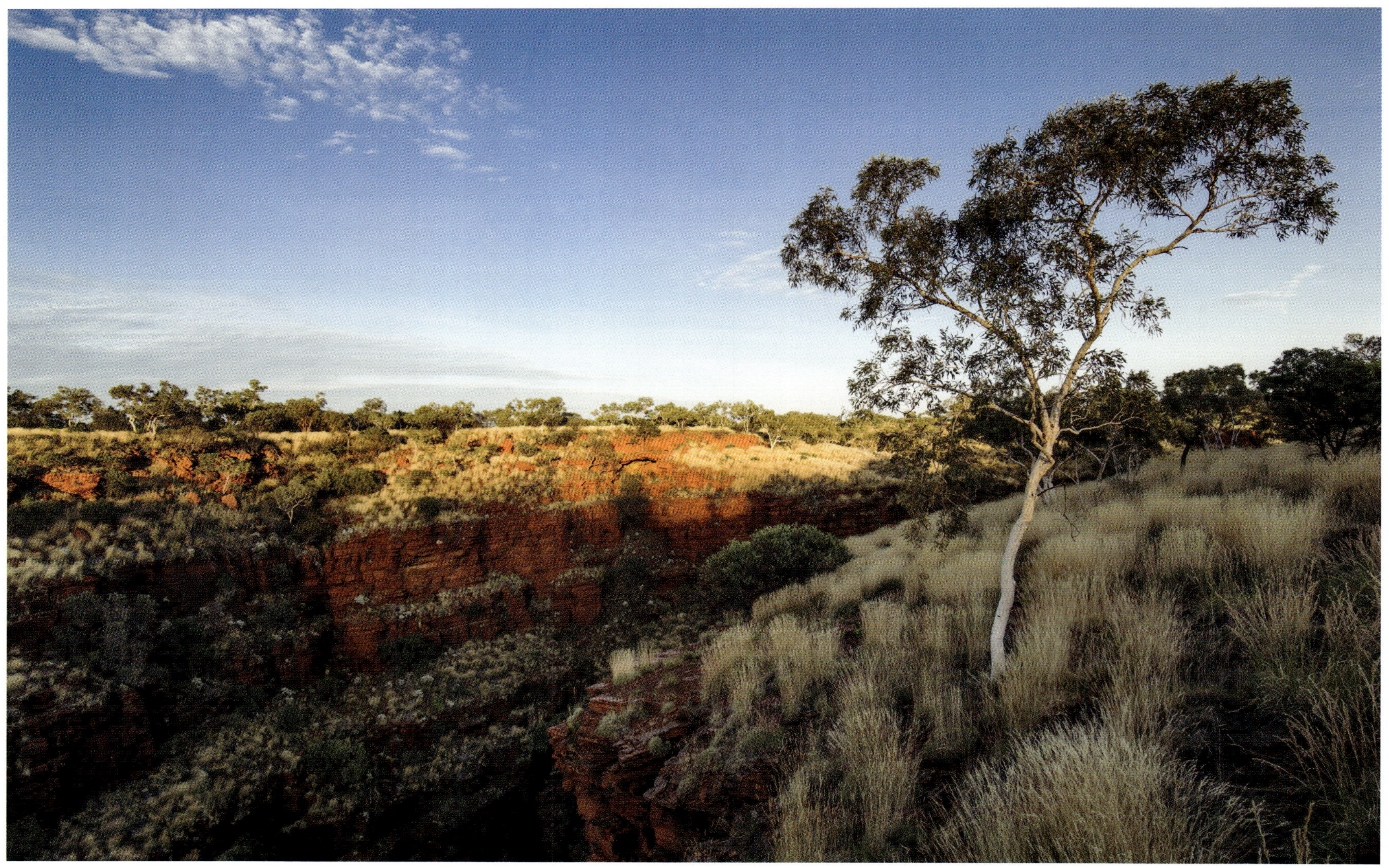

    KARIJINI NATIONAL PARK

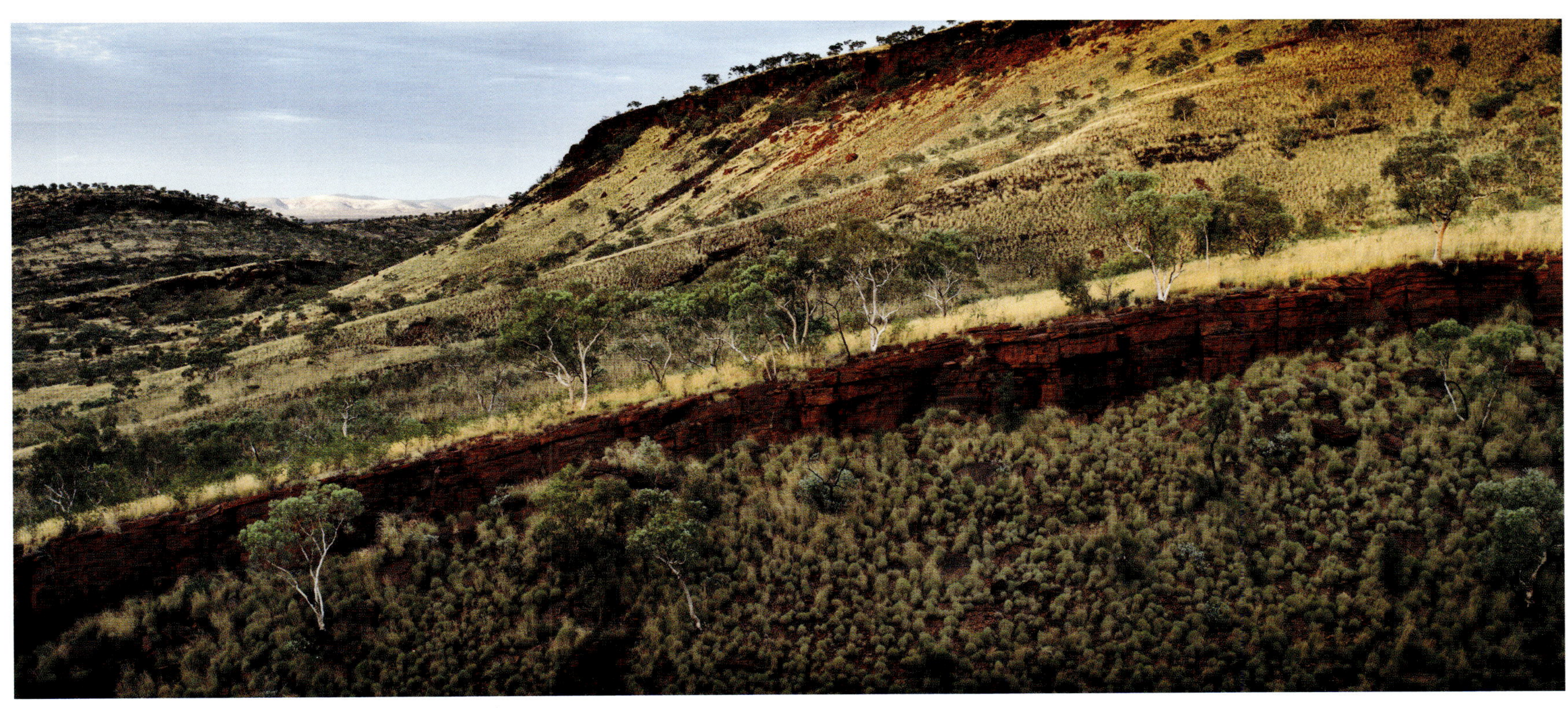

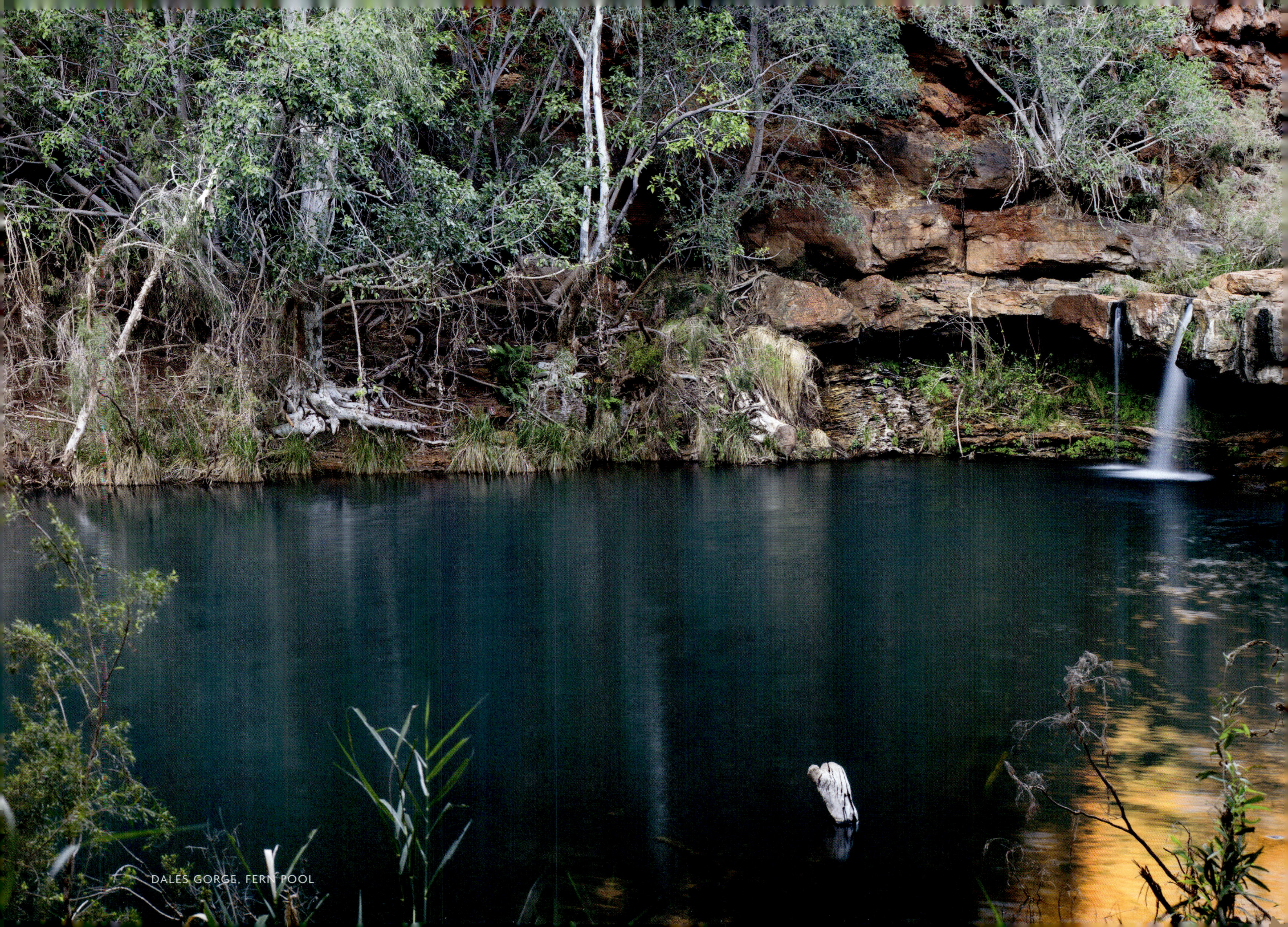
DALES GORGE, FERN POOL

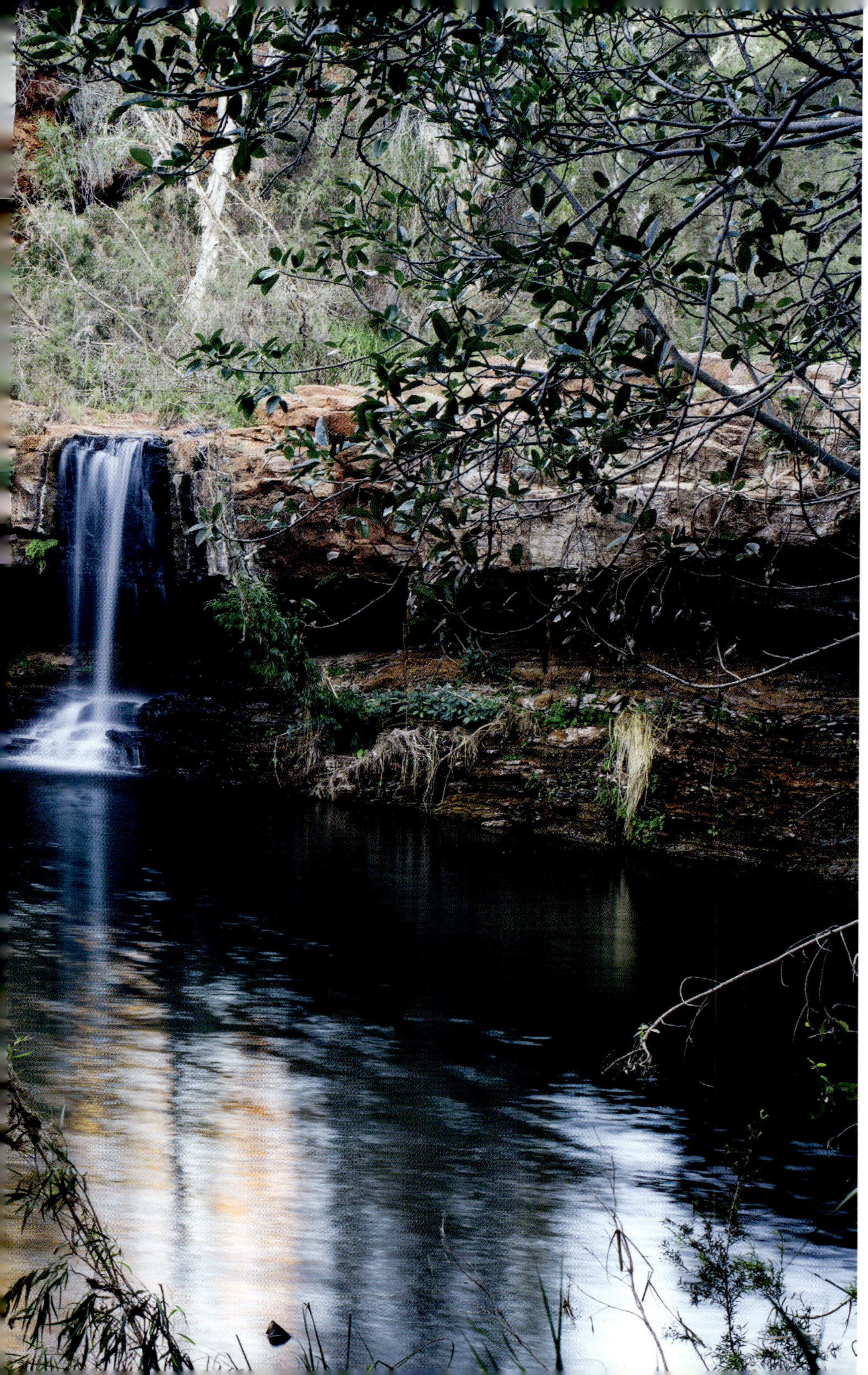

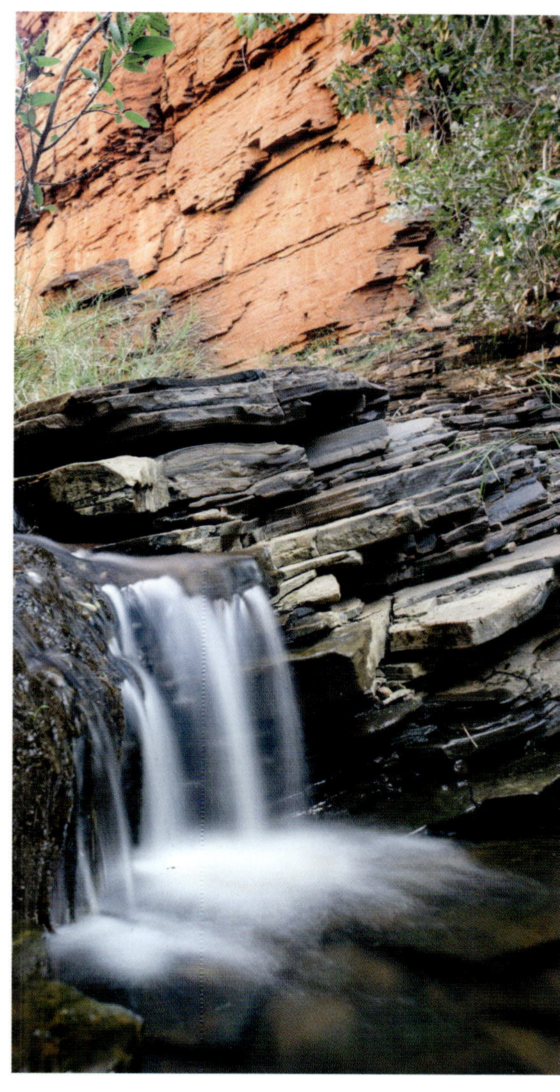

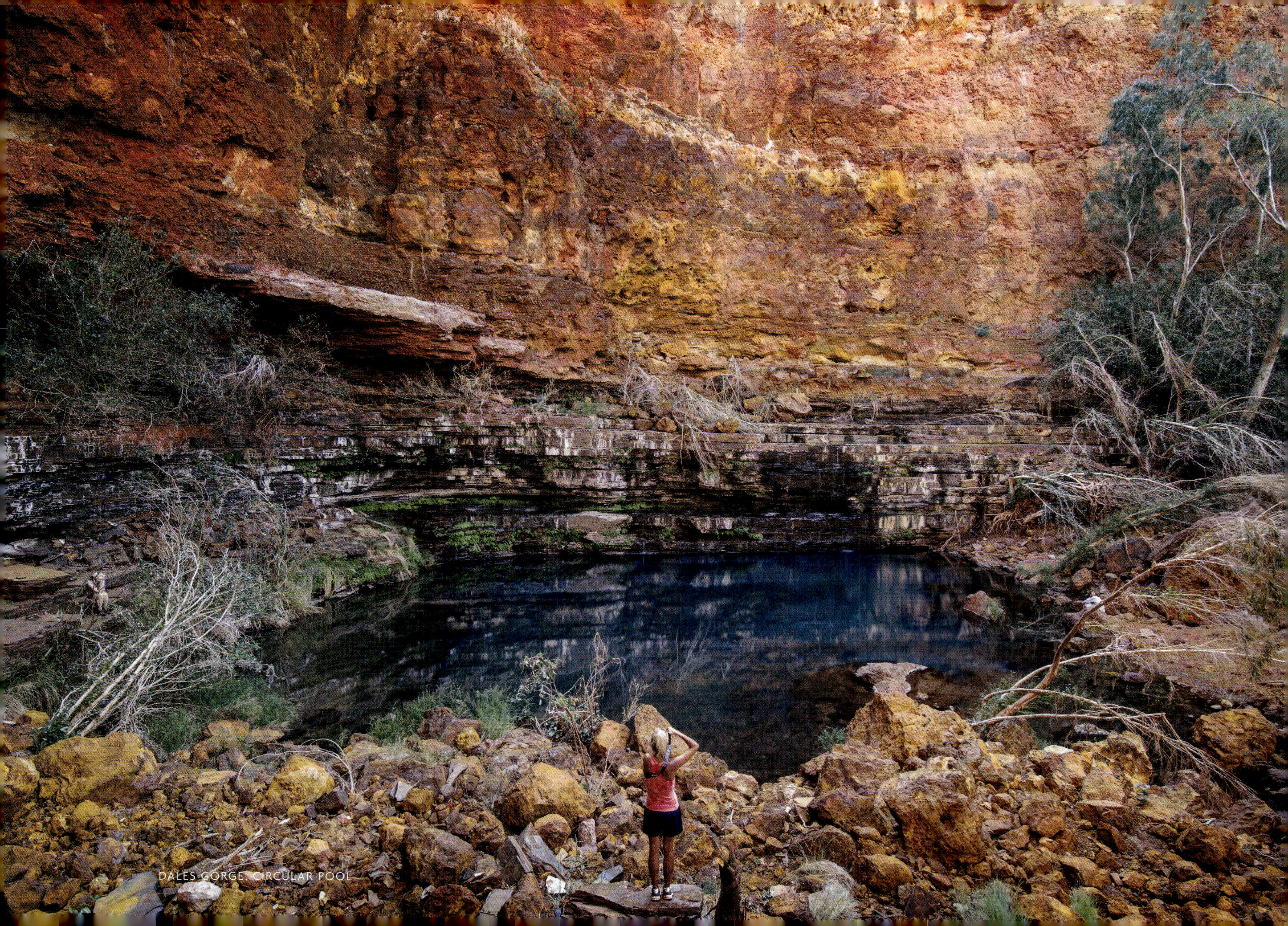

DALES GORGE, CIRCULAR POOL

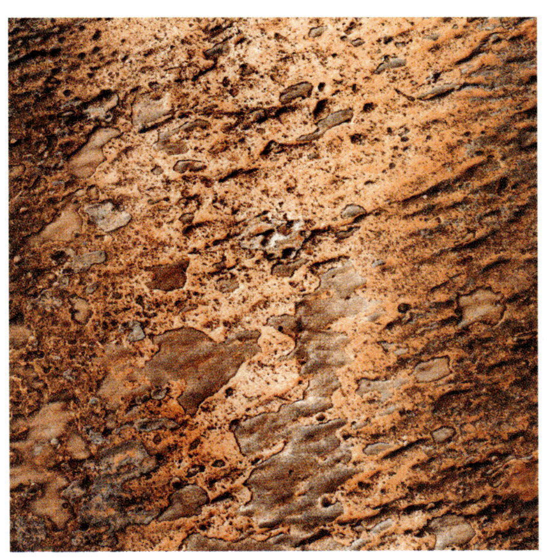 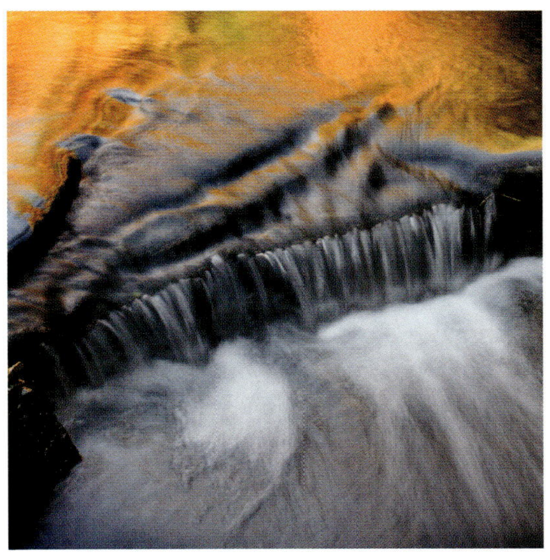 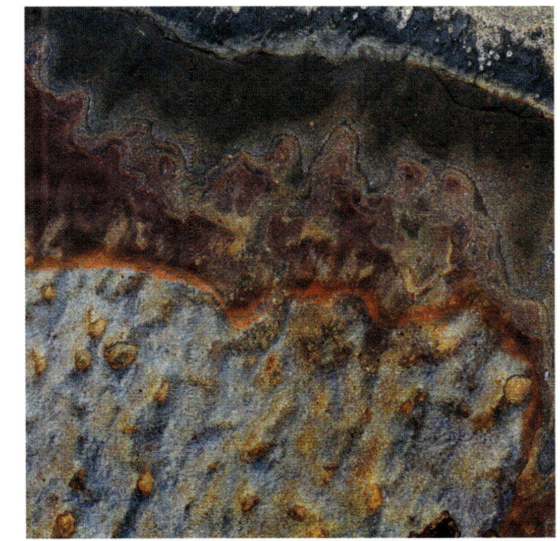

Dales Gorge's most popular attraction is its beautiful green Circular Pool surrounded by towering red walls and little waterfalls that emerge from the rocks. Temperatures in Karijini can easily hit 45 degrees celsius so a swim in this pool is absolutely mandatory.

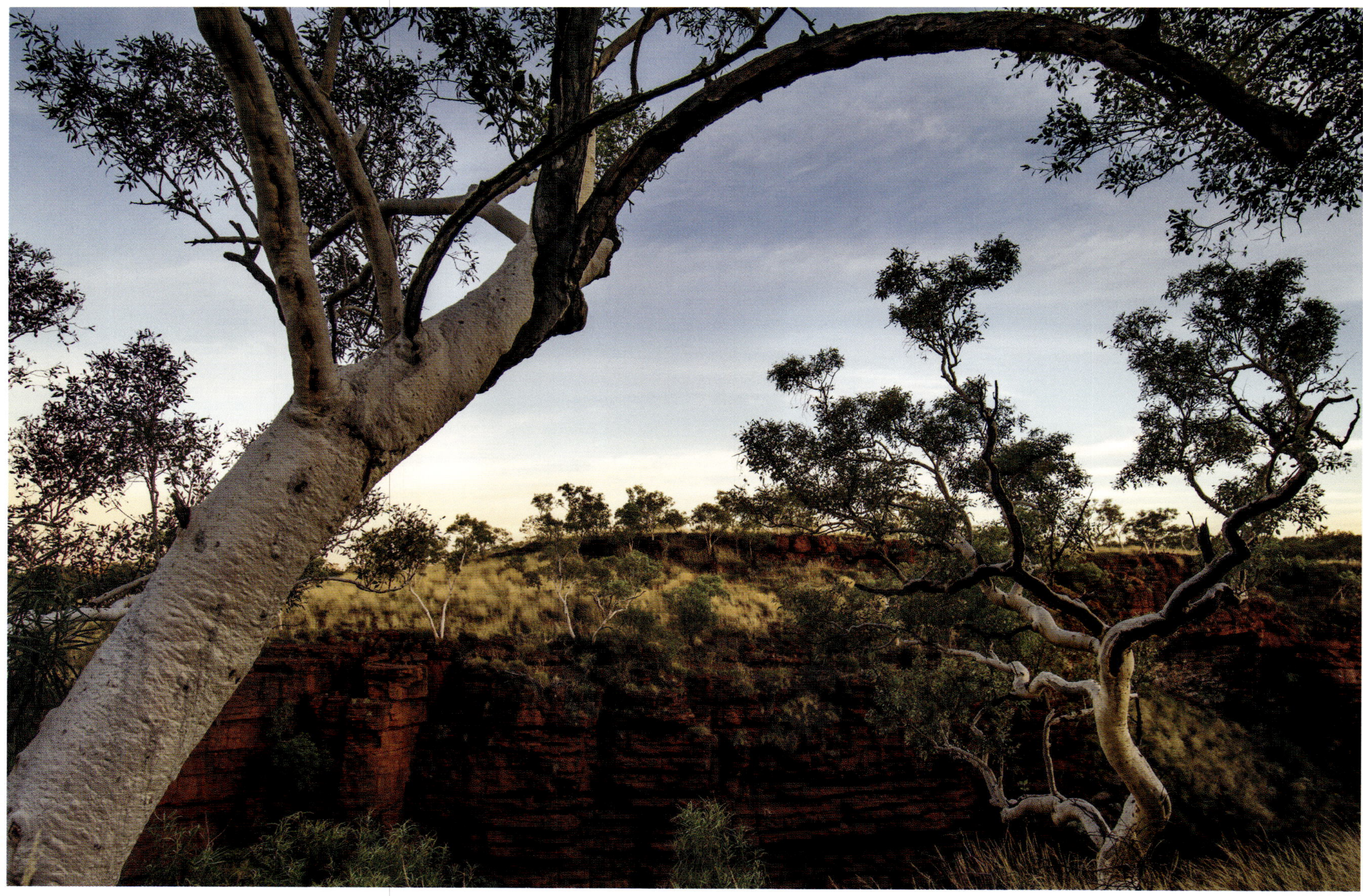

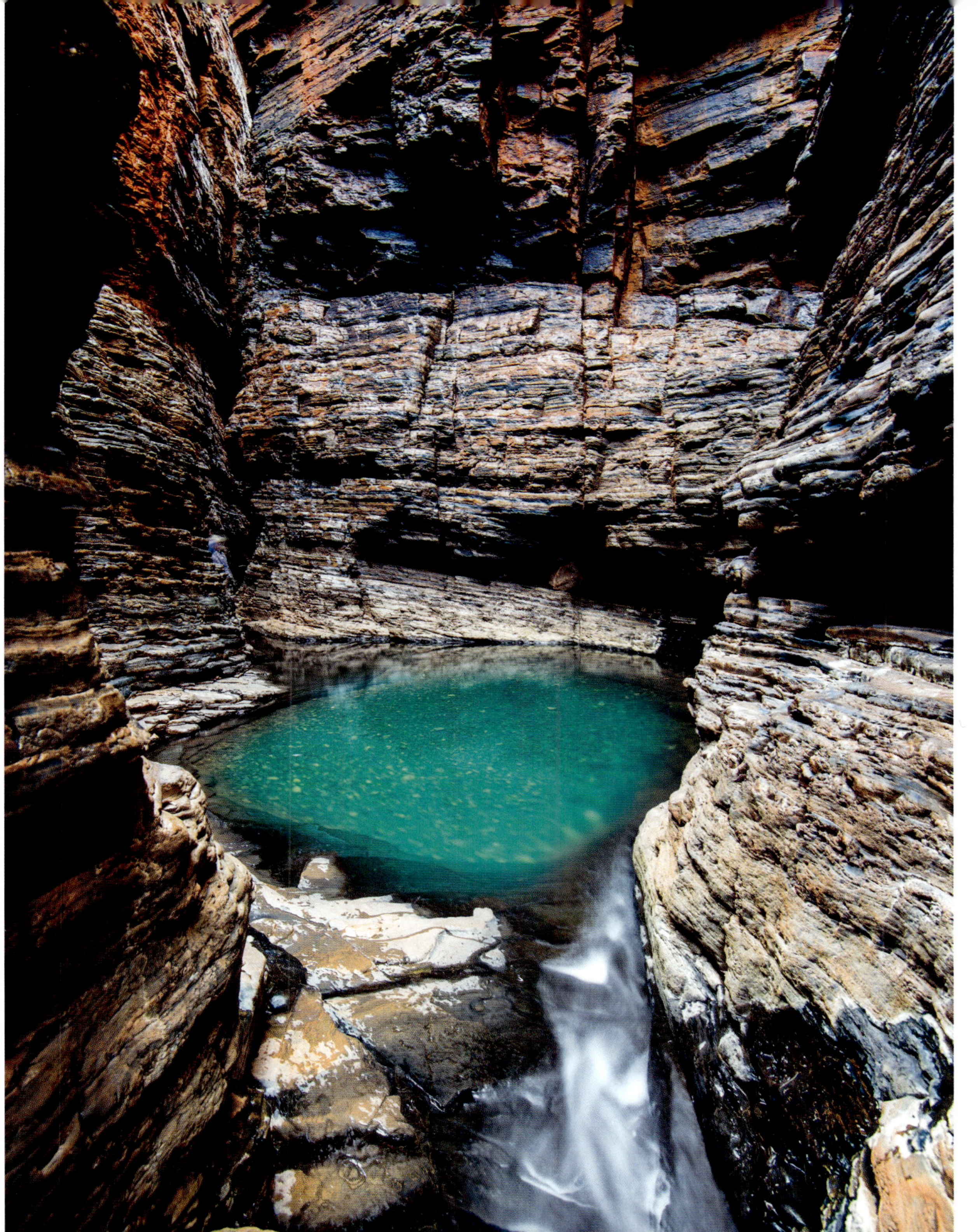

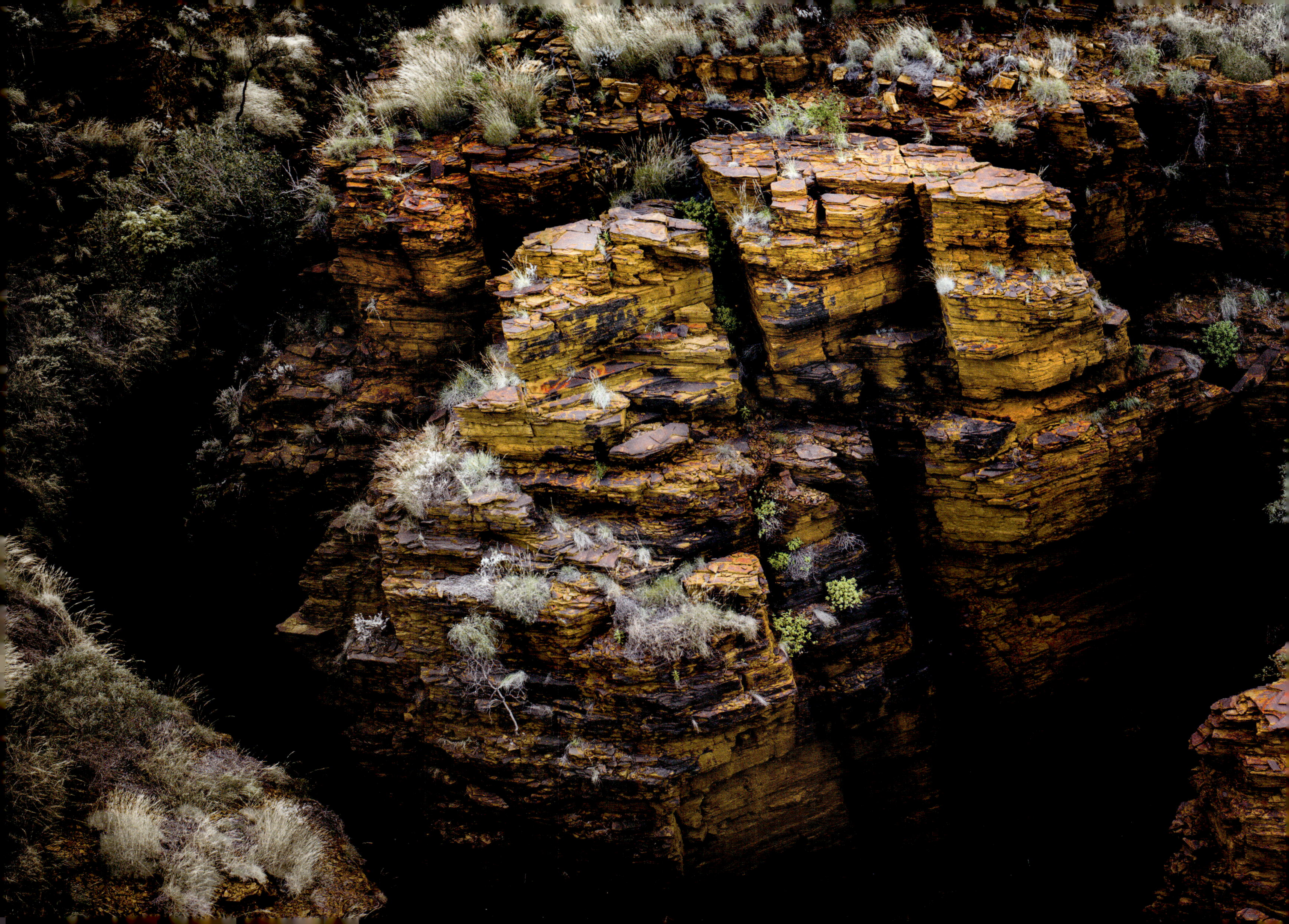

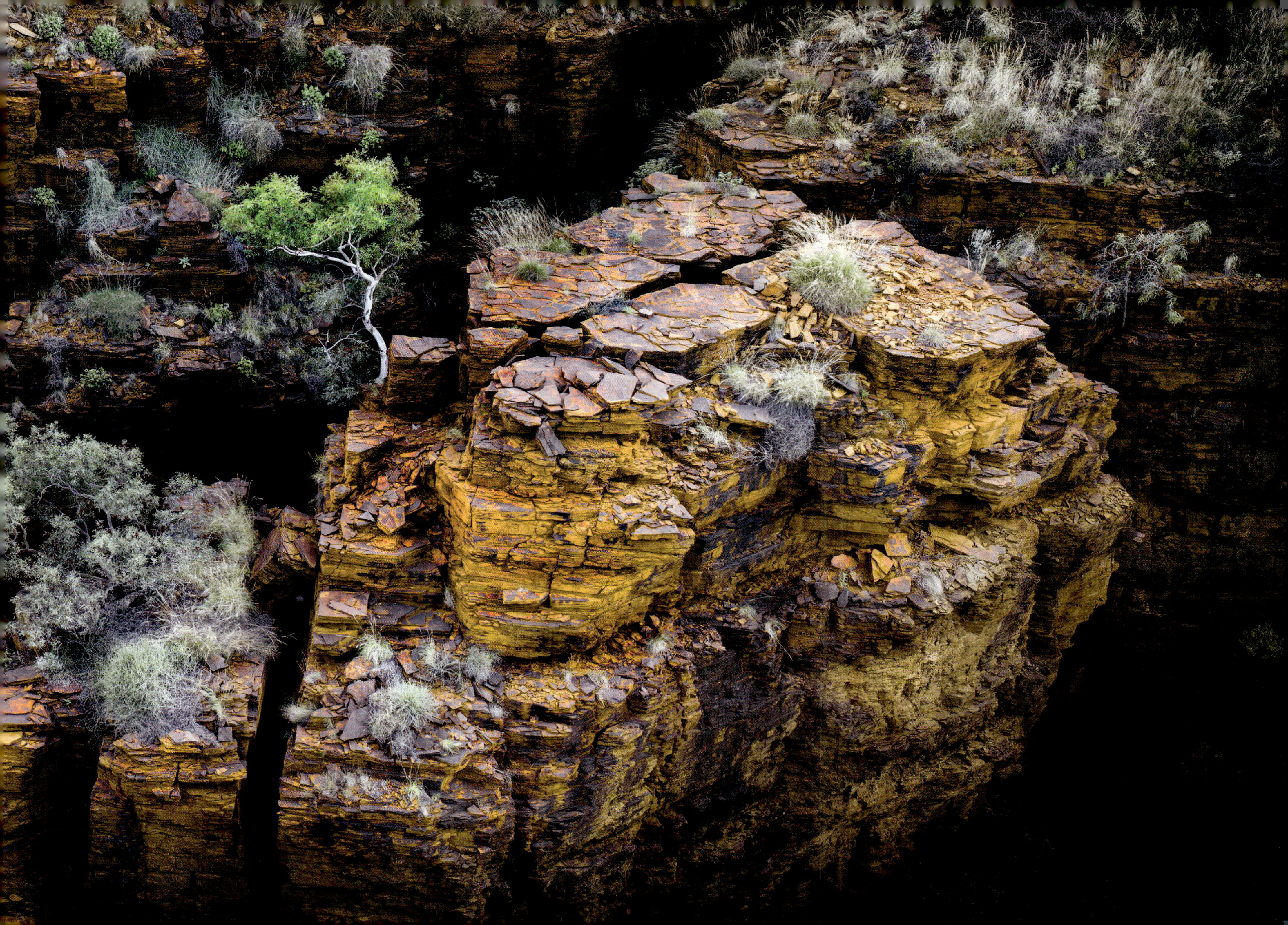

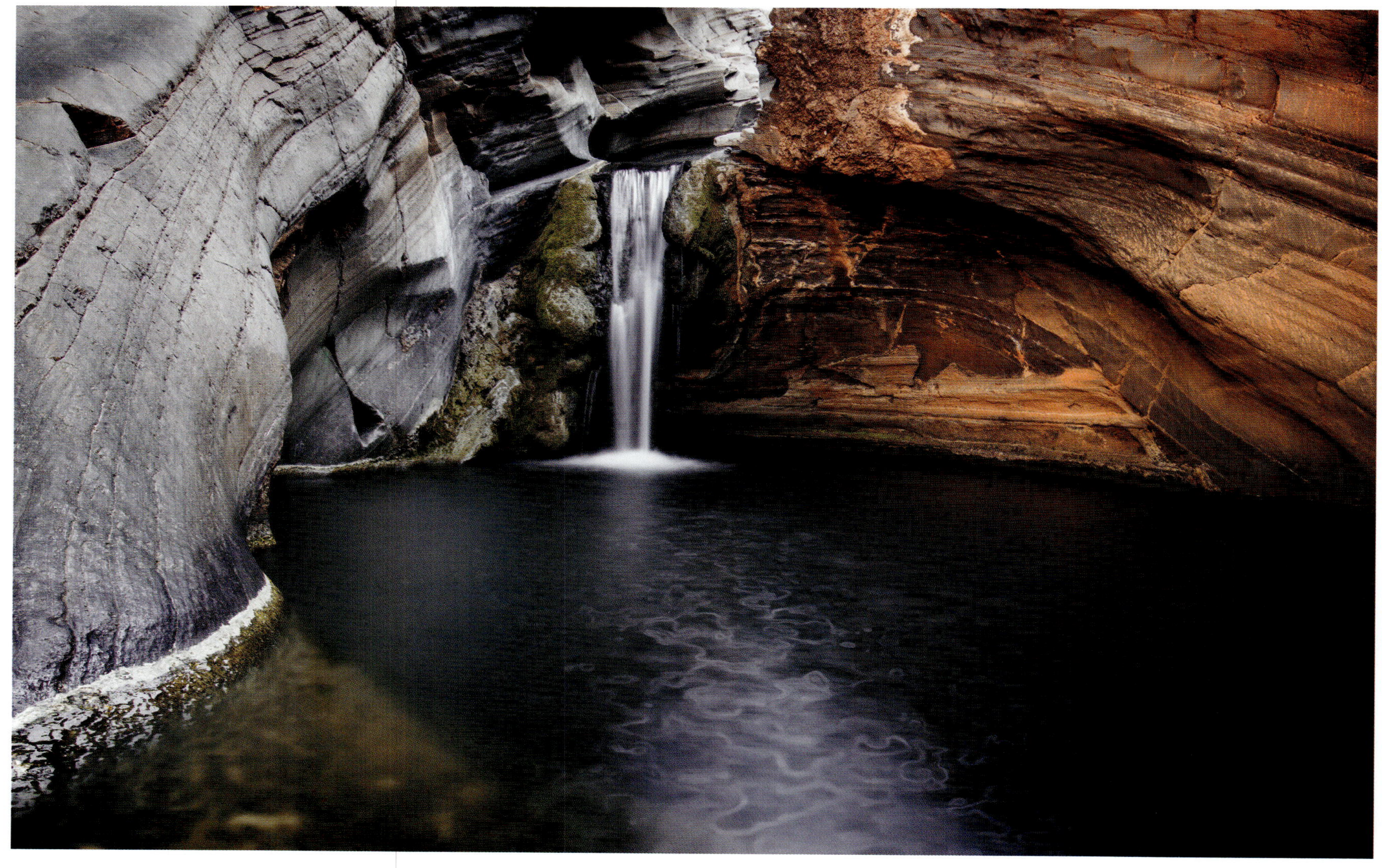

HAMERSLEY GORGE WATERFALL

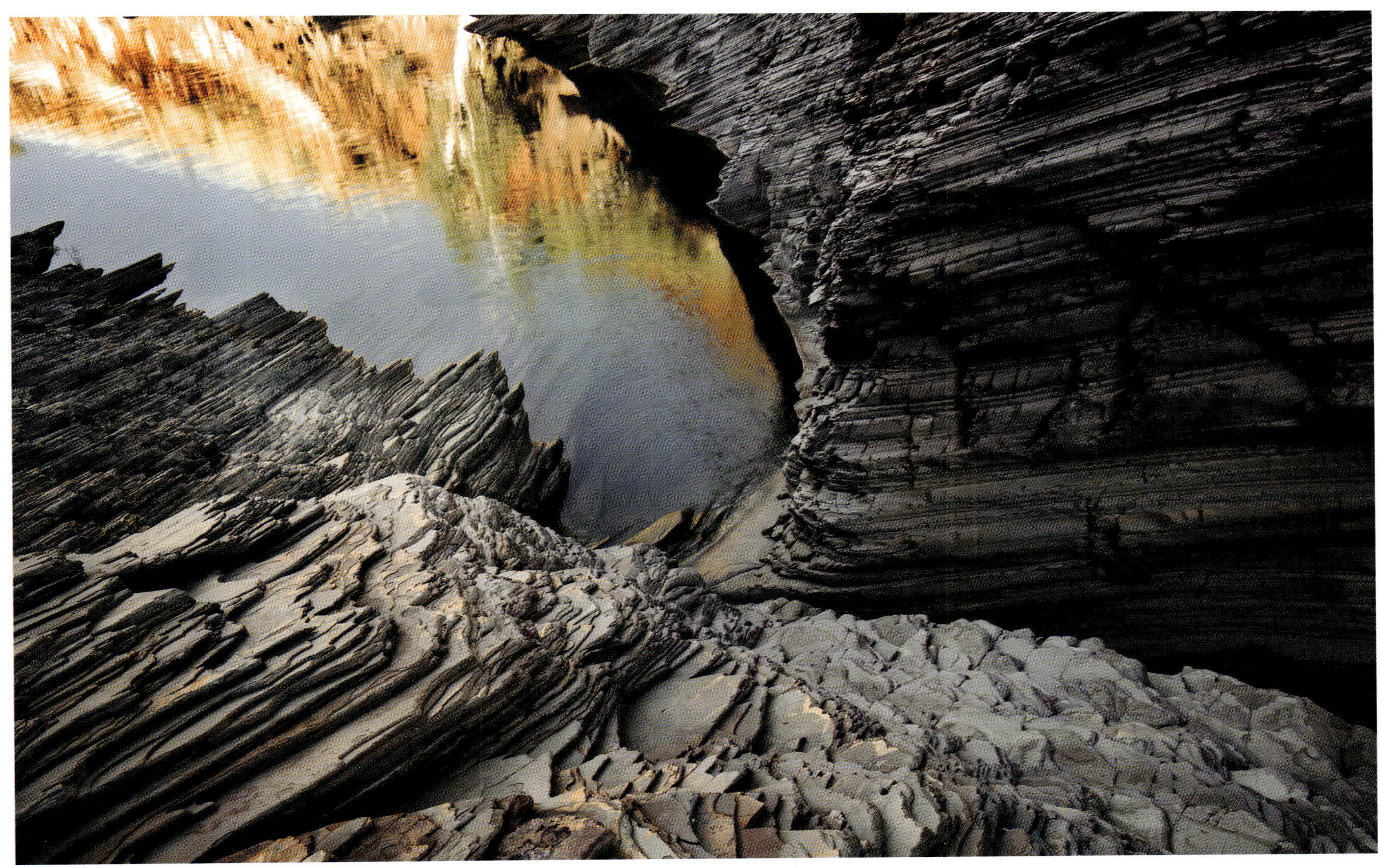

ACKNOWLEDGEMENTS

I would like to thank and acknowledge the following organisations for their contribution to this book

The Gumala Aboriginal Corporation

Western Australian Government; Department of Environment and Conservation

Western Australian Government

Tourism Australia

Tourism Western Australia

Western Australian Indigenous Tourism Operators Committee

I would also like to thank:

Amanda Hoyne and Staff at the Karijini Eco Retreat, Peter Eastway, Christian Fletcher,
Tony Hewitt, Siena Morrisey and Vanessa Wilton

Para Rafa y Leo

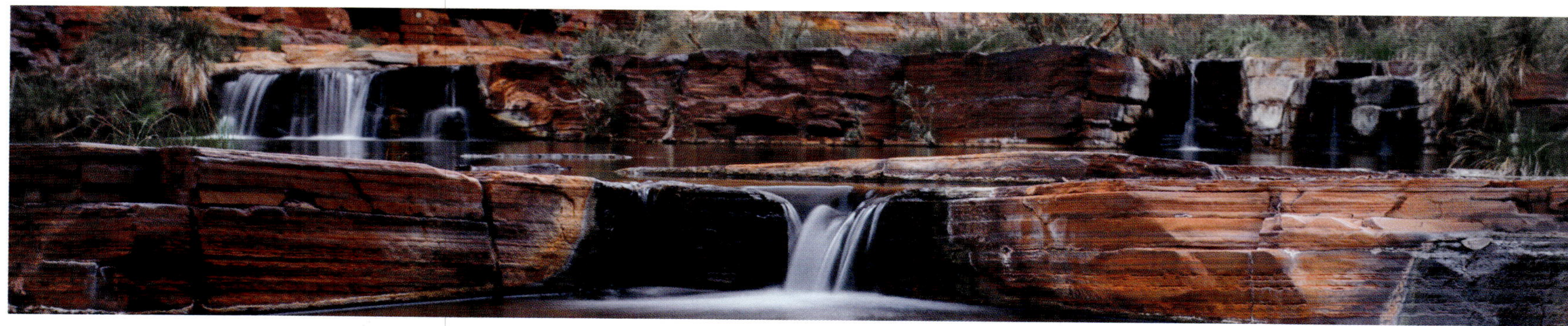

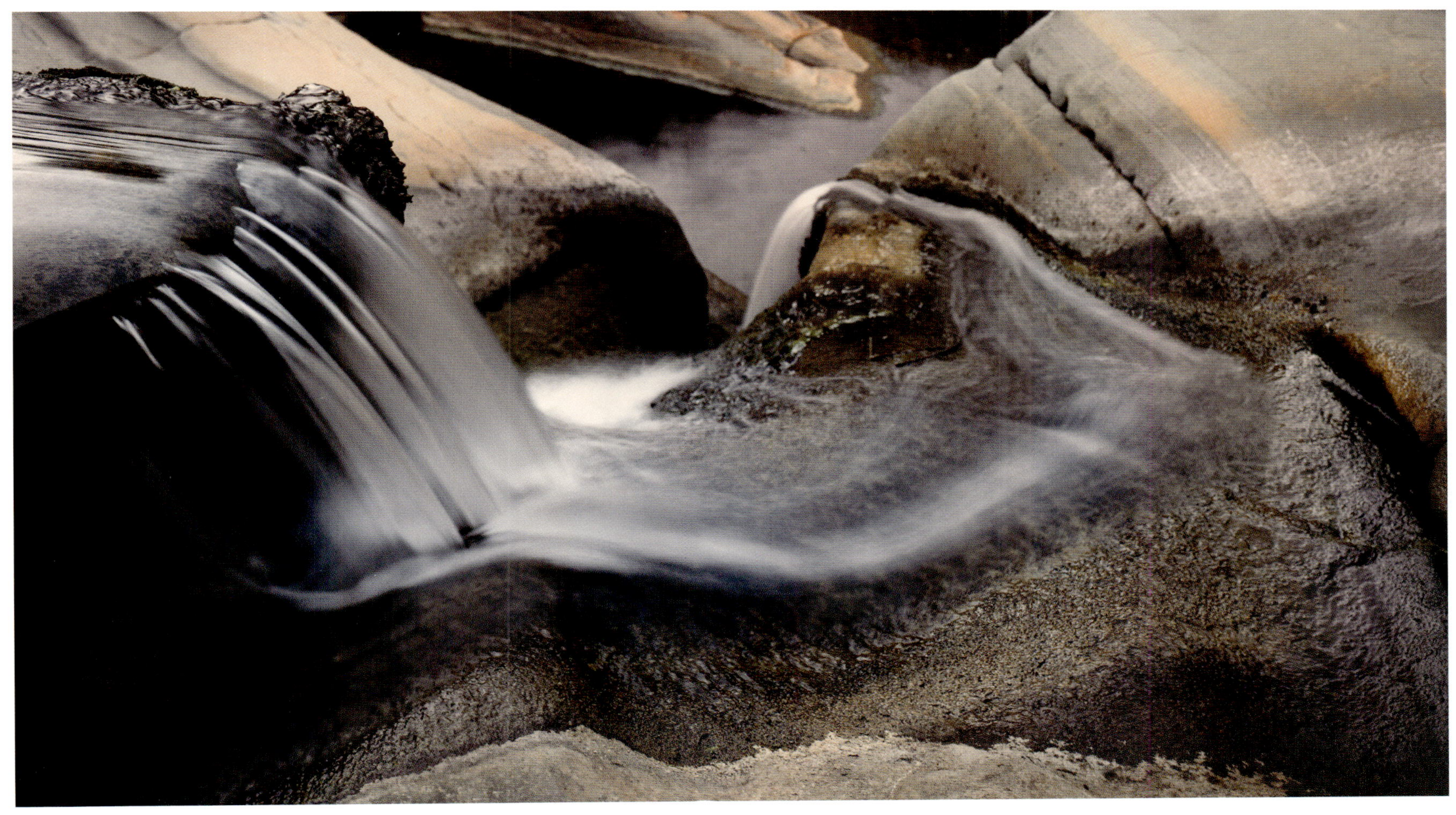

During my time in Karijini National Park, I stayed in the Karijini Eco Retreat, which is the first and only permanent up-market, luxury accommodation in the Park. The Eco Retreat is in a great location to access most of the best lookouts and gorges and has an excellent restaurant. Special thanks to my main sponsor, the Gumala Aboriginal Corporation, owners of Karijini Eco Retreat, proudly supporting the Nyiyaparli, Banyjima and Innawonga peoples of the Pilbara.

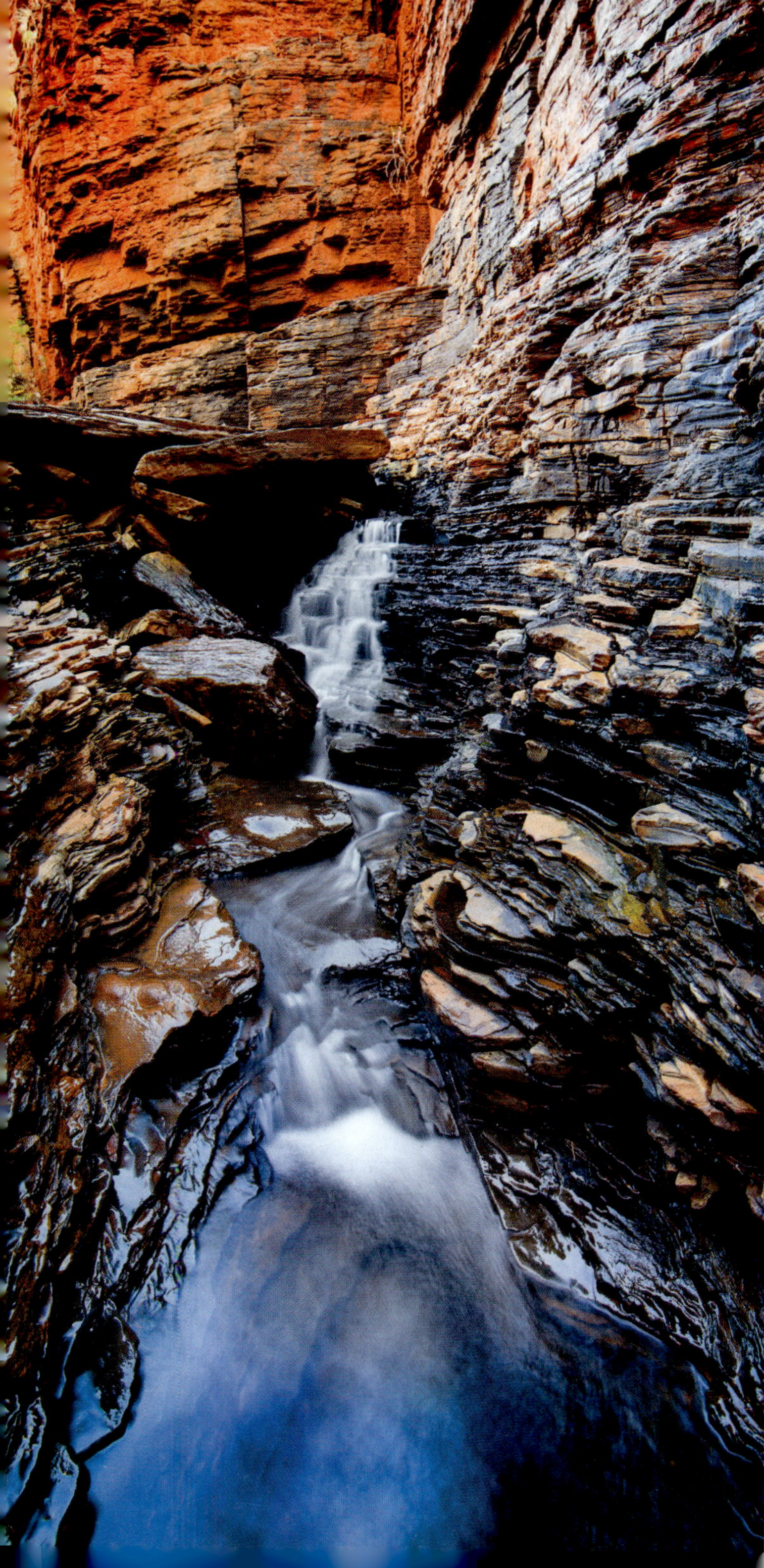

All photographs of the book were captured with a Pentax 645D medium format digital camera, high-end lenses and equipment for exceptional image quality. With 40 effective megapixels, this medium format camera produces extra-sharp, super-high-resolution images. At present I use both the 55 mm f2.8 AL (IF) SDM AW and 25 mm F4AL [IF] SDM AW lenses. I really enjoyed using the 25 mm lens. Incorporating two high-performance a-spherical optical elements within its optics, this ultra-wide-angle lens provides exceptional image-resolving power with outstanding brightness levels even at the edges, whilst keeping any aberrations to a minimum. I did not use filters but captured different exposures and merged them using PT Gui. All images were worked in Photoshop CS6. Other software used included PTGui, Helicon Focus and Adobe Camara Raw. For this purpose, I used a calibrated Eizo monitor CG241W.

Most photographs in the book were taken either at sunset or sunrise and using a tripod Gitzo GT1541T with a Markins head Q3 Emille Travel and a Really Right Stuff Sliding Panoramic package MPR-CL II Nodal Slide and PCL-1 Panning Clamp.

Some of the photographs in this book were exhibited in the Gaffa Gallery in Sydney in February 2013 as limited edition prints.